DATE DUE

BECOMING PLURAL

BECOMING PLURAL
A TALE OF TWO SUDANS

RICHARD BOGGS

Garnet
PUBLISHING

BECOMING PLURAL
A Tale of Two Sudans

Published by
Garnet Publishing Limited
8 Southern Court
South Street
Reading
Berkshire
RG1 4QS
UK

www.garnetpublishing.co.uk
www.twitter.com/Garnetpub
www.facebook.com/Garnetpub
blog.garnetpublishing.co.uk

First Edition

ISBN: 9781859642979

British Library Cataloguing-in-Publication Data
A catalogue record for this book is available from the British Library.

Design by Sheer Design and Typesetting:
www.sheerdesignandtypesetting.com

Printed and bound in Lebanon by International Press:
interpress@int-press.com

CONTENTS

To Ismael on the island

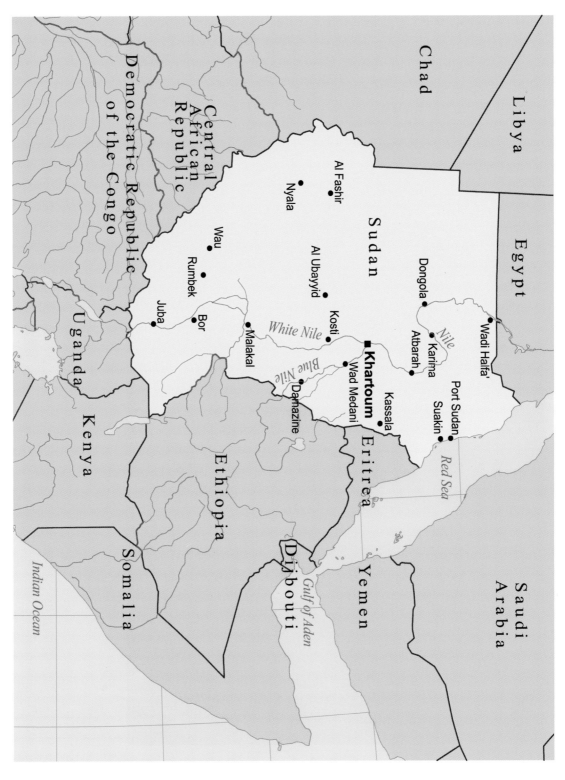

Sudan before July 2011

Ferry to the island, Kerma Mahas, Nubia

In the history of independent Sudan there has always been a persistent and pervasive assumption that Sudan was an Arab nation all of whose citizens would eventually adopt Arab culture, language and religion.[1]

1 Collins, Robert, *A History of Modern Sudan* (Cambridge: Cambridge University Press, 2008), p.137

CHAPTER ONE

ENCOUNTERS

Back in the colonial heyday in the 1930s, the artist Richard Wyndham found the Grand Hotel almost intimidating, as if he had entered 'the sacred portals of a club'. All was silence as the waiters walked barefoot among the guests, except for the chink of ice in gin and the rotation of the ceiling fans. The Grand Hotel was very, very grand. Nowhere, Wyndham concluded, could 'the white man's burden be more nobly borne'.[1]

From Khartoum, Wyndham travelled by train to Kosti, rather comfortable in his sleeper, and after enjoying his breakfast of kippers, declared the journey with Sudan Railways 'a luxury unknown in Europe'.[2] When his boat arrived in Malakal, the porters rushed up to the cabins, naked apart from a rope tied decoratively around the waist. Even the globe-trotting American lady on board gasped with surprise, if not admiration. Today, notices in the hotel changing rooms warn bathers of the need to 'respect Sudanese traditions' (Whose traditions are

SALVATION

I step down into the pool of the Grand Hotel on Nile Avenue and break the dusty film of its surface. Mahogany trees, trees General Horatio Kitchener is said to have planted when he rebuilt Khartoum, grace the Blue Nile beyond. Kites drift languidly on the air currents overhead: this is a city of kites and sparrows.

Already I'm breaking the law: there are two of us in the pool – with winter temperatures of 25 degrees it's too cold for the Sudanese – and the other swimmer is a woman. To ensure no hanky-panky in Khartoum waters, swimming times alternate with the hour, by law. In theory, even a husband and wife must swim at different times, although the staff turn a blind eye to all that.

For entertainment it's Abba this year, sounding out over the vast expanse of the empty pool, calling out for a man after midnight. Last year it was Celine Dion. A new year brings a new album.

1

those? I ask myself) and warn gym-users against any nudity while changing.

Things were also a little different when Frank Power, a correspondent for *The Times* of London, travelled to Khartoum to join the forces that were to fight the Mahdi rebelling against Turco-Egyptian rule. He wrote home in 1883 about the dress code of the day: 'After Berber, the natives (ebony giants) wear a knife strapped to the elbow as their sole clothing; the women natives, a five-inch fringe of blue and white china beads strung on thread.'[3]

Things have somewhat changed from the latter days of my youth when I was a volunteer in Sudan, and would take the ferry across to Tuti Island, then to Bahari to join the other bathers skinny-dipping in the Nile. When I first came to Sudan in 1986 there had been a sense of a country in crisis: basics were scarce in Khartoum and there were volatile demonstrations against shortages and the cost of living. But while others were waiting to buy bread, I'd be wanting to photograph the baker, all aglow in the warm light, setting out the circles of dough on the wooden plank that he would shove into the oven, withdrawing a minute later the thin flat circles of bread that are eaten with every meal.

The rule of Gaafar Numeiri had finally come to an end in 1985; a popular uprising forced his generals to

remove him and pass power to a democratically elected government with Sadiq al-Mahdi as Prime Minister. But things were falling apart: Sudan was on the brink, but we were not sure as to the brink of what.

As volunteers, we were fairly immersed in the culture, living like everyone else on the staple *fuul* beans – breakfast was *fuul* with salad, supper was *fuul* with cheese – but we were able to indulge ourselves on occasion. One June evening we treated ourselves to a night out in General Gordon's with a bottle of gin in a bucket of ice set on the table. Replete and in fine form, we hitched a lift in the back of a pick-up from Khartoum proper to Ondurman, and as we crossed the bridge over the White Nile, a colleague noticed that there were not the usual soldiers posted at such a strategic site.

Pot of *fuul*

'There are no sentries on the bridge,' he quipped. 'There'll be a coup tonight!' There was. That was my last public consumption of Ethiopian gin in Khartoum. The coup marked the coming of 'Salvation', for that's what the military regime came to call itself: Salvation.

THE VIEW FROM THE BRIDGE

As you travel over Omdurman Bridge you get one of the best views in Khartoum: the Blue Nile flowing from Lake Tana in Ethiopia, its waters divided by the green of Tuti Island, and the White Nile, seemingly more sluggish above the bridge, a vast expanse of water stretching to the horizon. The waters of the Blue Nile have lost some of their sediment on their journey but seem to flow with speed; the White Nile looks a more leisurely silty-grey. At the confluence, they don't immediately merge and the Nile retains a two-tone effect downstream. A traveller in the early 1900s wrote of the tendency of the waters to remain separate even after the Niles join:

[The waters of the two rivers never seem to blend ... the effect is that of dark, turbulent water rushing past a still lake of muddy white, and there is a distinct line when the waters actually meet. It is not until it gets some miles north of Omdurman that the water takes the colour which it bears on reaching Egypt – the colour of the White and Blue Niles blended.[4]

The British brought the iron bridge over from India I was told. You can stand there and watch the waters flow in a flurry of eddies, and see the 'Parliament' building and the Two Niles Mosque. Beneath the bridge there is an island – not Tuti Island, but a little island that is seasonally submerged then cultivated when the waters subside.

One day, I climbed down one of the ladders on the pillars of the bridge to the pumpkin fields of the island, fields the size of a room in a terraced house, walled with earth to catch the water pumped up from the Nile and tended by the hired labourers from the west who live in their straw *rokubas* on the Nile banks. This for me is the sound of the Nile: the 'putt, putt, putt' of the pumps rhythmically pouring their water into the irrigation ditches that define the fields, fields that mirror the sky in the late afternoon as they are transformed into clay-walled pools.

On the island you might catch a boat being loaded with baskets of aubergines, or hear a shepherd singing. In winter, farmers plough the rich earth that the Nile has yielded. With the rains, the island is flooded again and pelicans fish where oxen once ploughed. On winter days, the riverbanks are isolated, except maybe for a fisherman sitting by his net or the ashen-grey flap of a heron. On warmer days, men from the shanty towns come down to wash themselves and their clothes. Here and there, someone will be crouched down on an isolated rock, scrubbing himself down with a piece of net and some soap, scouring the pale soles of the feet with a stone, or standing on the shore, holding the loose *sirwal* trousers up above the head for a couple of minutes to dry in the breeze, his skin the rich black of the pendant aubergines that ripen in the fields by the Two Niles Mosque.

ARABIC LESSONS

When I first lived in Khartoum, teaching English at the Islamic University, I lived right in the heart of Omdurman. In the *suq*, women served tea in the alleys and men from the Gezira hawked coffee on great circular trays, going from merchant to merchant, the coffee kept hot by embers turning to ash among the *jabinas*.

The coffee-sellers would be up before the sun had risen over the brown landscape of Omdurman: the brown mud of the indigenous *jalous* houses, the house-walls coated with sun-dried dung and straw that kept the homes cooler in summer, the sky itself opaque when a dust-storm threatened. In some half-built concrete block they would be setting up the metal pots on the tray for the first customers of the day, the coffee

spiced with ginger, the little *finjan* or handle-less cup heaped with sugar. In those days, I didn't boil a kettle in a kitchen: the day began with a coffee shared with the labourers of the street.

My Arabic lessons were around the women who sell tea under the neem trees. The tea women of Sudan sit like queens in state, often fat and draped in their *tobes*, their throne a stool six inches off the ground.

Around the tea women are the tools of their trade: the charcoal stove of woven metal, the milk tins recycled as kettles to boil water, the tray of glasses heaped with sugar. They sit with authority as the men squat around, waiting for their tea or demanding another spoonful of sugar. Then the men argue over who should pay, each insisting that he should pay for the others, one pushing the other back as he reaches for the notes in his shirt pocket, 'I've sworn! I've sworn!' he calls, until his friend yields, and that's the excitement over for the day.

Before they knocked it down, the old corrugated-iron-roofed fruit and vegetable market in Khartoum was where I tried out my Arabic. There I'd drink coffee with the men who had gathered at the kind of hiring fair that took place under the scented neem trees, hoping for a day's work. It was there that I gave myself up to the rhythms of colloquial Arabic, absorbing the language of the *suq*, not the university where I worked.

Tea under the tree, Khartoum

Omdurman *Suq*

Around me, the traders would be seated high up above the fruit and vegetables in the market stalls, urging passers-by to purchase dates that were 'pure sugar' or oranges that were 'sweet as honey'. Or they would stand in their shops behind the various tins stacked with *fuul* beans or garlic, the beans a dusty pyramid in the glare of the sun.

Women would throw up their arms in feigned disbelief at the price being asked, then walk away, only to be called back with a more reasonable offer. And still she'd refuse, until the stall keeper would swear that she was offering less than he had himself paid. And as each harangued the other, you'd hear exclamations of 'W'Allah sa! W'Allah sa!' 'By God, it's true! It's true, by God!' It might even have ended with the stall keeper swearing that if he were not speaking God's truth he would divorce his wife.

I'd sit with the casual labourers of the *suq*, gathered around the *sheesha* pipe, the pipe passing from mouth to mouth. As the talk flowed and the bubbles streamed in the pipe, I'd be surrounded by the sounds of the market: boys selling single cigarettes, men throwing down watermelons from a lorry to be piled in a heap in the sun, fruit sellers urging passers-by to buy grapefruit and bananas and dates.

And so, apart from the interruption of morning classes, I idled away the hours from the first greetings of the morning to the last leisurely chat in the cool of the evening. My school was the *suq*: I learnt my Arabic among baskets of lemons from Tuti Island and tomatoes from the Gezira laid out on empty cement bags on the street, and baskets of aubergines from the banks of the Nile.

THE DETAILS

A faint acrid whiff sometimes hangs over the city. The brick-makers on Tuti Island fire their sun-dried bricks of Nile mud, insulated with a layer of smoking cow dung, in kilns on the riverbanks. This, for me, is the distinctive smell of Khartoum.

In the *suq*, Umm Ruwaba

The hennaed patterns on the women's ankles and on the backs of their hands, like delicately-leafed stems and swirling flowers, have a dusky intricacy. And the way the women hold themselves: they walk with grace but not with speed.

The traditional garment for men is the loose white robe that covers the entire body below the neck, the *jelabiyah*. Some have a pocket not just on the chest but on the back as well – there's no back-to-front in the traditional attire of the followers of the Mahdi. The traditional garment for women is the *tobe*, a loose robe in the colours of exotic birds: lemon, pink, crimson. Traditionally, the *tobe* was lightly thrown over the top of the head, leaving the hair partly revealed, à la Bhutto. Nowadays, there is the imported style, perceived as more 'Islamic', where the face is tightly framed with a dull wrapper.

The faces of the oldest men and women are sometimes ploughed with the scars that used to be cut into the cheek but are now rare. In the past, scarification would have been seen as beautification; the Victorian explorer Samuel Baker, travelling through Sudan in search of big game and the tributaries of the Nile, contrasted perceptions of beauty between here and the west: 'Scars upon the face are, in Europe, a blemish; but here and in the Arab countries no beauty can be

Brick kilns by the Blue Nile, Rosseires

The mark on the brow of the men, darker than the surrounding grain of the skin, is caused by the forehead touching the ground in prayer. They tend to pray outside on the pavement, the long prayer mat spread below the neem trees. Their faint perfume hinting of hyacinth is the other smell I associate with Khartoum. The shoes, those leopard-skin slippers that the merchants like to wear, environmental awareness being a little thin on the ground, are discarded in a line, the latecomers hurrying to join one of the bowing rows.

perfect until the cheeks or temples have been gashed.'[5] Scars are the obvious marks of tribal identity: cuts like the number 111 or a 'T' carved into the cheek according to the ethnic group, but today this is more a characteristic of grandmothers at a wedding than Sudanese youth. There is still a wealth of scarification among the Southern tribes however: deep cuts across the brow; a ring of beaded flesh along the forehead; thousands of dots swirling over the entire body.

Western dress, unfortunately, is more popular than before, except for Fridays when it's traditional white for the mosque. The men's shirts fall over their polyester trousers, never, apart from those in uniform, tucked in beneath. In Khartoum, you cover your ass.

The taxis are yellow, the shutters and doors of the shops are green, and the city is a dusty brown. Khartoum: drab city by the blue of the Nile in the intense light of the desert sun. But some of the streets are picturesque, with the tea drinkers gathered by the *zeers*, the clay pots of cool water shaded by the branches of the waxy banyan tree that frame the scene. Taxi drivers idle by their cars, both cars and drivers often looking over half a century old. The drivers tend not to go looking for a fare; they wait for the fare to come to them. Some stretch out indolently on cardboard on the pavement in the midday heat; people here tend towards the horizontal.

Prayers at the scene of the *mulid*, Omdurman

When the men greet each other, one arm extends to tap the other person on the right shoulder, and then there is the embrace or the slapping of the other's shoulder, and a warm handshake. In Sudan they have their own Arabic.

'Inta tamam? Mea mea? Shadeed?' 'Are you fine? One hundred per cent? Are you strong?' And the one greeted, as they continue slapping each other on the back, is bound to reply:

'Mea mea, al hamdillah!' 'I'm one hundred per cent, thank God,' even if he felt anything but.

GENERAL GORDON AND ALL THAT

Khartoum came about because of an incident at a feast. When the Turks were attempting to establish their control over Sudan from Cairo, the local chief, Mak Nimer, butchered the lot while they were feasting in Shendi rather than submit to their rule.

It was this incident that marked the birth of Khartoum. The ruling Pasha, Mohammed Ali, having revenged his son's death with a general slaughter of the Sudanese, established Khartoum at the confluence of the Niles. From here he would try to control Sudan, the main source of slaves for their armies.

The history of Sudan is very much bound up with its northern neighbour and with the military conquest of Egypt. The British influenced Sudan through Cairo, but with the general insurgency against Turco-Egyptian rule led by the Mahdi, the Awaited One, they wanted to abandon Khartoum, for their interest was Egypt, not Sudan. The issue was not unlike the one facing western powers today: how to withdraw from an occupied country without losing face. General Charles Gordon was sent to do just that: to evacuate Khartoum. However, rather than playing the game and withdrawing, he refused to abandon the population of the garrison town.

The correspondence Power smuggled home to his family in Dublin show how at least one of the besieged

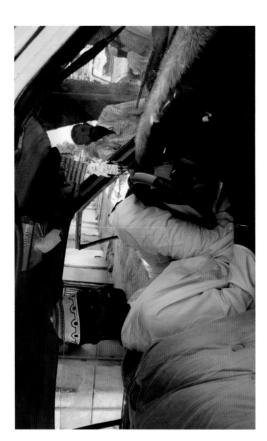

Taxi driver, Khartoum

When the British explorer Wilfred Thesiger arrived in Khartoum in 1935 it was the expat life that appalled him:

Khartoum seemed like the suburbs of North Oxford dumped down in the middle of the Sudan. I hated the calling and the cards, I resented the trim villas, the tarmac roads, the meticulously aligned streets in Omdurman, the signposts and the public conveniences.[6]

He went off to Darfur instead, hoping again for Ethiopia's 'colour and savagery, hardship and adventure'.[7] But suburban North Oxford? Obviously Khartoum has somewhat changed since Thesiger's day.

empathized with the enemy forces surrounding the city. 'I am not ashamed to say I feel the greatest sympathy for them, and every race that fights against the rule of Pachas, backsheesh, bribery, robbery, and corruption.'[8] Power may have been a 'monocled and sardonic observer of war,'[9] but he saw the Mahdi's cause as an honourable one.

Power did not have a lot of faith in the garrison forces defending Gordon's Khartoum, writing that they had 9,000 incompetent infantry who could be routed by fifty good men and 1,000 cavalry who had never learnt to ride.[10] He was eventually evacuated from Khartoum, but the steamer went aground before it reached Dongola, and Power was killed when he accepted a local sheikh's 'hospitality'.

Power's perspective, with a westerner identifying with the indigenous, is the exception rather than the rule, although the British Prime Minister William Gladstone also sympathized with the rebelling Sudanese. More typical among western writers is the portrayal of the Mahdi as the Oriental despot, rather than the leader of a people fighting for their freedom. Winston Churchill is different. Rather than falling for the discourse of Orientalism and portraying the Sudanese as either voluptuous sensualists or religious fanatics, Churchill sees the Sudanese rebellion as primarily a social revolt, with the Mahdi bringing together a people rebelling against the injustices of Turko-Egyptian rule.

They were also rebelling against the justices of that rule as Britain forced Egypt to act against the slave trade. In tackling slavery in Sudan, Gordon had helped bring about the movement under the Mahdi that would drive out the forces of occupation and allow slavery to be restored. Attempting to stop slavery in Sudan was to undermine, as in the American Civil War, society itself.

Not all Europeans in Sudan had qualms about slavery: the Bakers enjoyed a life-long relationship which began when the explorer spotted Florence in an Ottoman slave market in a Bulgarian town and bought her. More disconcerting was the Swiss explorer Johann Ludwig Burckhardt who, travelling in Sudan in 1814, documented the horrors of slave-trading in Sudan, with each caravan from Kordofan filling the market in Shendi with slaves. On the domestic scene, however, he concluded that 'slavery, in the East, has little dreadful in it but the name.'[11] He bought a slave, a boy of 14, in Shendi 'for the sake of having a useful and constant companion' but also as an ostensible reason for travelling to the Red Sea, where he could sell the boy for a profit.[12] Burckhardt took turns with his slave to ride the camel he had also bought, an arrangement that must have raised a few eyebrows among his fellow travellers. Arriving in Suakin with his clothes in rags, he sold the camel at a considerable loss; concerning his travel companion I found him silent.

It was difficult for the British to keep their hands clean as they dealt with Sudanese and Egyptian rulers. Not unlike the delicate question today of Afghan rulers and opium, Britain had to reconcile governing with dealing with rulers whose main interest was obtaining slaves. Gordon was pragmatic: despite his drive against slavery, after one of his mystical moments he decided the man to save Khartoum from the Mahdi was the greatest Sudanese slave-trader of the day, Zubehr Pasha. This option was unacceptable to the British government; Gordon didn't get Zubehr and Khartoum was lost.

The protagonists in the Khartoum drama are, of course, the Mahdi, Muhammad Ahmad bin Abdallah, a boat-maker's son from Dongola, and General Gordon, from Woolwich, son of a Major-General. In this apparent 'clash of civilisations' on the Nile, the main protagonists are actually rather similar, both leaders being military mystics, with the Sudanese leader perhaps more orthodox in his beliefs than the Englishman.

Gordon refused to surrender for 317 days,[13] only to be 'martyred' on the palace steps when the Mahdi's forces took Khartoum, if paintings dramatizing the event are to be believed. It was one of those rare occasions when the British, as opposed to the Sudanese, did not turn up on time. Having outsourced the transportation of the troops as far as Wadi Halfa to Thomas Cook, and then negotiated 120 miles of broken water at the rate of one mile a day (they had 1,500,000 tins of bully beef to load and unload daily)[14] the rescue mission arrived two days too late. Today, Gordon on the Nile seems not so much a tragedy as the material for an entertaining musical.

With the death of Gordon, the Mahdi briefly ruled Sudan from Omdurman until he succumbed to typhus. In his wish to overthrow corrupt governments who served imperial powers, we can see parallels in today's Middle East. His Islamic state would have gone far beyond the borders of Sudan; he threatened Empire itself. Was the Mahdi a role model for a Saudi who lived here as a guest of the nation in the 1990s? (As his dangerous liaison with the Sudanese authorities came to an end, Bin Laden left Sudan in 1996 for Peshawar and Afghanistan without getting paid for his construction jobs.)[15] Any Sudanese I have spoken to have utterly rejected the comparison, protesting, I think, a little too much.

It's tempting to imagine Bin Laden contemplating his future at the tomb of the Mahdi, but devotions at a tomb would have gone against the tenets of Salafism, although tombs are very much a feature of the landscape and centres of religious devotion for the Sudanese. More important, the mysticism that the Mahdi embraced would have been anathema to Bin Laden's dour sect. But in their charismatic personalities, their denunciation of corrupt, superficially Islamic governments and their fusion of religion and politics to take on world powers, to a non-Sudanese like me it does seem that Bin Laden and the Mahdi had something in common.

When the Mahdi died, his successor, the Khalifa Abdullahi, declared Omdurman 'the sacred city of the Mahdi' and built the Mahdi's domed tomb right by the Khalifa's house. Like many a Sudanese I have visited the tomb, and chatted with its genial guardian, who told me with delight how his own grandfather from Darfur had joined the Mahdi's forces who despatched Gordon.

We can get a sense of what Omdurman was like at that time from the accounts of an Austrian officer who had converted to Islam. Colonel Sir Slatin Pasha got to know the sacred city well as he was a special 'guest' first of the Mahdi and then of the Khalifa. Slatin presents the Khalifa's rule as tyrannical, with even the

Sheikh's tomb near Dongola

haji to Mecca forbidden, the Mahdi's tomb substituted as a place of pilgrimage.[16] From Slatin's descriptions of the refuse in the streets, it seems Omdurman, unlike Austria, was not a place where cleanliness was next to godliness. Slatin finally escaped after 12 years of captivity, smuggled across the desert to Aswan, where a band playing the Austrian national anthem escorted him on to the postal steamer bound for Luxor.

The Khalifa ruled his Islamic state from Omdurman, until Gordon's death was avenged by Kitchener. With the killing of 10,000 Sudanese at the Battle of Omdurman

The guardian of the Mahdi's Tomb with his son

Kitchener's gunboat *Al Milek* at the Blue Nile Boat Club

The Mahdi's Tomb, Omdurman

Annexe at the Khalifa's House Museum

in 1898, it was hardly the even playing fields of Eton as British machine guns fired on sword-carrying Dervishes, the technology of Europe wiping out the indigenous tribesmen. Churchill reported that Kitchener thought the enemy had been given 'a good dusting';[17] today there would be calls for a war crimes' investigation. Sickened by the slaughter of the Sudanese, Churchill's verdict on the 'liberation' of Omdurman was that rescuers had never been more unwelcome.

Kitchener shelled the Mahdi's tomb from his gunships, and had the remains dumped in the Nile – like Bin Laden, the Mahdi had a watery grave – to prevent the further growth of a cult around his burial site. Barbarically, Kitchener kept the head for a time as a trophy. You can still find one of Kitchener's gunboats, *Al Milek*, almost forgotten among the bougainvillea of the Blue Nile Boat Club. Standing by its tiny hulk of metal sheets riveted together, I had to acknowledge the heroism as well as the barbarism of those times.

Khartoum was re-built on a more imperial scale, the streets set out in the form of the British Union Jack. Typically, the city was planned in a suitably stratified manner, with the upper-class residences near the Nile; the further from the Nile, the lower the social class and the greater the heat. The Sudanese were beyond the pale in Omdurman.

Khartoum today is three distinct towns. There is Khartoum proper with its government buildings, rather shabby but not without elegance, and its once grand avenues. Then there is Bahari in the north, both green and industrial, with its remnants of boatyards. And, finally, there is Omdurman, with its extensive *suqs*, the metal doors all painted Islamic green, and dusty lanes where the Sudanese mill around in their traditional *tobes* and *jelabiyahs*. By the Nile you can still see the Mahdi's tomb among the palms.

CONFLICT AND IDENTITY

During those years when I first lived in Sudan, I observed the country being transformed. There was a conscious Arabization and Islamization, so that Arabic alone became the medium of instruction and there was a much greater assertion of things Islamic, especially in the 'jihad' against the South. As with so many other wars it was largely about oil, with scorched earth policies in some areas to give the oil companies a free hand, but the war was definitely packaged in the language of 'jihad'.

There had scarcely been a time since its independence in 1956 that Sudan had not been at war, going from coup to peace treaty to coup and war again. The British

Khartoum street scene

Omdurman Suq

withdrawal from Sudan had been a fairly peaceful one, for it was Egypt that mattered, and their rule in Sudan did not generally have the vicious oppression that marked their rule in Kenya, the Battle of Omdurman and the suppression of uprisings excepted. Even as the British were preparing for departure, it was not just the nature of the new state that was unresolved, for the country itself had yet to be defined: would Sudan be an independent state or would Sudan and Egypt form one country? The Sudanese opted for an independent Sudan, but how could a country with over 100 languages – reading a list of Sudan's ethnic groups is like skimming through a page in a telephone directory – ever be a successful nation-state, especially one where the North was dominated by Arab-Islamic traditions and the South by animist-African traditions?

If borders tend to reflect the language, religion and cultural practices that a people hold in common, a supposition much less true of Africa than of Europe, what sense do Sudan's borders make? Given that there is such a wealth of cultural diversity, what do the Sudanese have in common? What 'makes' someone Sudanese, apart from having been born within the borders of a state drawn up by colonial powers?

The Polish journalist Ryszard Kapuscinski poses the question as to how these apparently incompatible worlds

Portrait in Malakal

Portrait in Malakal

— the 'Arab' Sudanese of the North and the African Sudanese of the South to put it in simplistic terms — could co-exist within the borders of one state. The answer for Kapuscinski was simple: they could not, and that was exactly what the British wanted. They would formally give up Sudan, but *de facto* continue to govern it, being 'needed' to reconcile warring factions.[18]

Conspiracy theories aside, 'There is no North without the South!' was the slogan repeatedly chanted when I lived in Omdurman. The imposition of *sharia* law, or rather a version of it, by Numeiri in 1983, was the final straw for the Addis Ababa peace accord that, with its relative pluralism and recognition of some of the rights of Southerners, had allowed the South considerable autonomy. The agreement was ditched for Arabization and Islamization and the result, of course, was a return to war. What Southerner whose beliefs were animist or Christian would want to accept the status they would have in a Sudanese 'Islamic' state?

It is these issues — the question of identity, the insistence on imposing a version of *sharia* law not only on Muslims but on all Sudanese citizens, and the control of the oil reserves — that have been the major sources of conflict in Sudan. Concerning identity, neither pan-Africa nor pan-Arab movements have united Sudan. With the coup in 1989, which brought Umar al-Bashir, backed by Hassan al-Turabi, to power, there came a perceived solution: Sudanese identity lay in Islam. I have heard one of my ministry trainees say it in a formal presentation: 'Religion unites Sudan.' Of course, given my own Irish background I saw things rather differently; in both Sudan and Ireland identity defined by religion has been a major source of conflict. But my trainee was talking more of an aspiration than a reality; for him, when 'non-Muslim' Sudanese converted to Islam, Islam would unite the country.

My ministry trainees were the most delightful of people. But in the 1990s, at least, there was an extreme Islamist ideology in government circles by which Southern Sudanese were portrayed as *kuffar* and therefore legitimate targets; this word defined them as non-believers who, according to some, should convert or be legitimately killed. According to the writing I have read on the walls of Juba, two million Southern Sudanese died as a result. Four million were displaced.

Back in those heady days of the late-1980s, a country on the periphery of the Islamic world set out to become the heart of an Islamic world that it would re-create. *Sharia*, of course, was enforced in a way, but it seemed to me that Khartoum was not so much under Islamic as under martial law. The historian Robert Collins compared the 1989 coup to a gigantic *haboub* (a great wall of dust blowing in from the desert) that swept away 'all hope of a secular, democratic and united Sudan.'[19]

MY THATCHERITE YEARS

If youth is wasted on the young, I wasted mine, not behind a desk in an office in pursuit of a pension, but indolently living for the day with the Sudanese. Work filled up that time of the day between breakfast, a rather late event in Sudan, and noon prayers. I was in the field of education where, with the initial enthusiasm of the 1989 coup, the baby was being thrown out with the bath water.

Everything would be in Arabic, even at university level, where the vast majority of texts are in English. Over two decades later, Sudan is reaping the rewards of such policies, and many a doctor does not have adequate English to study abroad and many a graduate leaves university with a Bachelor of Arts but an elementary level of English.

In such a situation I was someone very much going against the grain of things: a Christian (with a very,

very small 'c') teaching in an Islamic institution where I was well treated, a foreigner where almost every other teacher was Sudanese or Egyptian, a teacher of English where English was being consciously rejected for Arabic.

I led a double life, teaching in the university in the mornings and learning in the *suq* in the afternoons. Indeed, even between classes I would nip out and breakfast with the mechanics working in the industrial area next to the campus, and dip into the communal bowl of *fuul*, much preferring their company to that of the academics. Mornings were spent teaching English language and literature. As villages in the South were being bombarded from the air, I was teaching a little Shakespeare in Omdurman. 'Shall I compare thee to a summer's day?' has a somewhat different ring in Khartoum, where May heralds not darling buds but sandstorms, soaring temperatures and a sky laden with dust. No Sudanese would want to be compared to a day in summer: even when the words used are the same, it is culture that determines understanding.

Weekends were often spent in the more dubious areas of the city, savouring another life. In the outskirts of Omdurman the rooms would be lit by a wick stuck in a tin can, and the Nuba would consume *marissah*, their grainy beer, for some a breakfast staple.

Vendor in Damazine Suq

The regime's version of *sharia* was imposed on everyone, whether Muslim or not, and this led one day in Ramadan to my having a little encounter with the authorities. In the *suq*, a lad in a wheelchair had read my mind and asked me if I wanted something. We went to one of those rundown houses behind the cinema where they used to sell *araquay* and the like, where dubious types wearing trainers would enter one of the dilapidated rooms and disappear for a while. After a short time, I left satisfied, but was stopped by a policeman in the street who called out irately.

'I know you! I always see you around! What are you doing here?'

Indeed I had broken the law: I had eaten a breakfast of *fuul* beans and bread. It wasn't enough for the Muslims of the North to fast; everyone had to fast with them. In those days, even the domestic water supply seemed miraculously to go off during the Ramadan day. Fortunately, just at that moment a friend came by in her car, and I jumped in and waved goodbye.

At the grassroots there could be a different code of behaviour. Another Ramadan I made the mistake of travelling in the back of a lorry along the road – then more like a track – between Atbara and Abu Hamed in the scorching sun. And there, long before the sunset call to prayer, someone pulled me into an almost empty café and gave me tea, and I had bread fresh from the baker's and juicy tomatoes. And that's what I remember about Abu Hamed: the hospitality shown towards me on the road, although I did wait over a week for the slow, slow train to Wadi Halfa.

Decades later, when I returned to Sudan in 2006, after years in Syria and the Yemen, I found it in some ways changed, for things had, at least superficially, eased up, but essentially Khartoum was just the same. With the boom years that came with oil, however, there had been considerable development of the infrastructure

In the bakery, Rosseires

of the capital, and the bridge to Tuti Island was soon nearing completion. I asked one of the men working on the bridge if he would mind if I took his photo, for I wanted to document it all. It was not just Khartoum that had somewhat changed, however, and he reminisced.

'I remember you!' he laughed. 'I drank *marissah* beer with you years ago in Omdurman!' And then he used a very Sudanese word, *laziz*, which is used to describe more than just a meal that is tasty.

'Why, you were a delicious youth back then!'

ON TAKING PHOTOGRAPHS IN SUDAN

Once, in the Gezira, the wide plain between the Blue and White Niles, I caught sight of some tribesmen from the east with their herds near the market in Wad Medani. And I asked one of the young men if I could take his photograph, for even in Sudan it isn't every day that you encounter such beauty: the comb through the wild hair, the dark waistcoat over the *jelabiyah*, the sword worn at the waist in its leather sheath. And he agreed, gladly, for some of the men are not without a certain vanity.

But as I took my photographs, someone interrupted my pursuit of beauty, demanding to know why I was taking a photograph of the dirty water in the street. I hadn't noticed the water, of course; we have ditches at

home and I hadn't come to Sudan for that. But surely he must have known that it was a portrait that I was taking. Did he for some reason feel ashamed of my subject's lack of modernity?

When it comes to photography, Sudanese officials have a certain paranoia. I suspect it comes from the 1980s when Darfur was hit with famine in the last years of Numeiri's rule and Sudan was overrun with westerners taking endless photographs of emaciated babies, preferably held in the arms of a celebrity. Numeiri of course denied that there was a famine, and even after his departure I was told that it was illegal to say the word 'famine', although 'drought' was a permitted word.

The permission to take photographs issued by the authorities states what you cannot photograph: beggars and bridges and, quite naturally, military areas. But the reality is that on any occasion a camera is produced, someone in plain-clothes may intervene. Surely the Sudanese don't have an underlying sense of shame about their own culture? Or is there a belief that if something cannot be documented in a photograph, its existence can be more easily denied?

It happened in the Omdurman *Suq*. I was doing the usual expat thing, taking a photograph of the handicrafts, the little funnel-like tin *jabina* pots that are used to serve up coffee. I had asked the seller if I could take the shot, but a middle-aged man came running up in consternation.

'What are you doing?'

'I'm taking a picture.'

'And where is your permission to take photographs?'

I reached into my camera bag for the form that gave me permission to photograph Sudanese customs and beautiful scenery.

'Why are you taking a photograph?'

'I didn't realise this was a military area!' I replied a little sarcastically. He immediately put me right on that issue.

'All Sudan is a Military Area!' From this good man's perspective, the definition of military area went far beyond the army camps.

'Could you just say that again, just to make it clear for me?'

'All Sudan is a Military Area!'

Well, who could argue with that? Winston Churchill, who had participated in the Battle of Omdurman in 1898, had written of two Sudans. The true Sudan, for him – but not for me – was the South: 'The real Soudan, known to the statesman and the explorer, lies far to the south – moist, undulating, and exuberant'.[20] Then there was the other Sudan, 'which some mistake for the true', stretching from the Egyptian border to Omdurman. This was the Military Sudan, with limited natural resources but a rich history of war.

Had anything changed since the days when Churchill had witnessed the last major cavalry charge of the British Empire? I was living in a country where, with the remnants of what had been called a jihad still surviving, even secondary school girls went to school in a fetching uniform of a tunic of light blue camouflage over trousers. But in a state with so many men in uniform, with the uniformed police looking rather gorgeous in plain turquoise, there were also a significant number like my photophobic, xenophobic speaker of

Metal handicrafts, Omdurman *Suq*

English working in some plain-clothes capacity: a major source of employment in Sudan. This was just one of the contradictions of Khartoum; while the 'detectives' could be a contemptuous lot, I found that the men in blue always treated me with civility and decency.

The Military Sudan! Could I argue with a statesman like Churchill? This was a country where about three-quarters of the budget was spent on and by the military, while trivial pursuits like education and health were each allocated one or two per cent. I put my camera back in the bag and walked away; you had to be careful taking photographs in the Military Sudan.

LIVING ON THE SURFACE

Once, in my first year in Sudan, I travelled by train to Darfur. Like other discriminating travellers, I opted to journey on the roof of the train. The passengers on the roof are actually the discerning travellers, what with the view and the company. With my first-class ticket I had shared the compartment with 15 others (there is a Sudanese proverb which says that the river doesn't refuse more) in intolerable heat. On the roof there was space and the occasional whiff of a joint somewhere being passed from mouth to mouth. I was up there with the *shammasha* — those who live their lives in the

sun, in the streets — and the sociable soldiers who share a blanket in the cold nights on the roof and all those who wished to travel free and enjoy the view.

Sometimes an unfortunate first-class passenger will catch sight of a roof passenger falling past the window. If the roof passenger falls to the side of the train he might just brush off the dust and jump on the train again, such is the pace of travel. My trip to Darfur took three days, but it takes much longer now. And there was the freedom then to walk through the orchards of the mountain, from village to village, although that is out of the question now.

It was not a journey for the faint-hearted, sleeping among my fellow passengers across the train roof at night, hiding from the heat of the sun by day. And so I became one of the *mesuttayeen*, those who ride on the roofs of trains and buses, who are on the top, on the surface. The word is also used by the streetwise in Khartoum, those who sell clothes and watches from stalls in the streets, to describe those who live merely on the surface of life, who are green and ignorant and do not have an in-depth knowledge of things.

I lived in Sudan for years but was really only on the surface of Sudanese life. With a superficial knowledge of Arabic, but a good command of the colloquial, and government permits allowing me to travel to certain places, I managed to capture some of what was on the surface. I was like someone who could photograph the iceberg above the surface, but knew that what was of real interest lay below.

A RACE AT SUNRISE

Once, when I was flying to Khartoum from Istanbul, I played a game with the Sudanese guy next to me and his Turkish guest.

'Can you think of five things to do in Khartoum?' he asked. That game occupied us for the rest of the flight.

There aren't many monuments to see in Khartoum, apart from a tomb or two. Basically, apart from the national museum, you can do the sites in an afternoon. In Khartoum you have the Nile and the Sudanese, and that's about it. It's the Sudanese themselves who are the attraction.

One thing you can do, however, is visit the camel market in Omdurman. When I lived in Omdurman, they still raced their camels down one of the dirt streets at *Suq a Naga*, the Market of the Female Camel. There would be great excitement as the riders raced down a line of men then tried to bring the camel to a halt before the road became a T-junction. The real races were on Fridays at dawn, when boys of nine or ten raced the camels across the desert and the owners chased them in Toyota pickups to select the best for export to Saudi Arabia and Kuwait.

I once managed to talk the sheikh into taking me with him to the Friday races. I left on a Thursday evening in the back of his four-wheel drive with his relatives, Hamid, Hamid, Hamid and Adam; there is not a lot of variety in the names the Sudanese give their offspring. These were nomadic people who were now settling down to life in the outskirts of Omdurman.

The house where I stayed was a room with a couple of beds and a new rug on the dirt floor, the rug probably having been brought out especially for me. There was no running water but the first signs of electricity were making their presence felt: on the floor were a car battery and a portable television. About 20 men and boys sat in the near dark, the television being the only source of light in the room. And so my first night with the bedouin of the desert was spent watching an Egyptian soap opera.

Before sunrise we set off in the sheikh's four-wheel drive with the boy jockeys wrapped in their blankets shivering in the morning air. As we drove through the desert, the sun just rising above the horizon, I caught a glimpse of another life: solitary men walking their camels in a desert landscape in the cold, clean morning light, a life that seemed to be fast disappearing in favour of soap operas and Toyota pick-ups.

At the starting place, there were maybe half a dozen pick-ups lined up, and before I knew it, we were off: the jockeys whipping the camels into action, the vehicles tearing after the camels, with myself in the back hanging on for my life as the sheikh's four-wheeler bumped its way across the sand. There was great exhilaration in it all, but what was it like for the jockeys, rising and falling on the saddles as the camels raced across the sands?

ROMANCE IN THE DESERT

One Friday I took a guest, an English doctor, not to the races but to the camel market. You could tell she was new in Sudan; she walked with a purpose.

The whole visit to Mwele, on the outskirts of the town, was, like so much else, a bit of an anti-climax: Mwele and its camel market seemed to be just a few huts and the wind blowing in from the desert. The camel owners must have sensed my disappointment for they promised us some amusement. When one of the camels was untied, I wondered what the nature of the entertainment was going to be: a race across the desert perhaps?

Beja tribesmen racing camels near Port Sudan

As the camel approached a female that sat hobbled on the ground, the possible nature of the entertainment dawned on me. The male began to make great gurgling noises and I hoped that the bedouin, who have perfected hospitality, were not now going to commit a social indiscretion. As saliva dripped from its mouth, the male started to hump back and forth on the female, which had little choice in the whole business, being still tied with ropes. I turned to see how my guest was responding; surely a doctor would not be offended by such an anatomical act?

Desert romance in the cinema is one thing: the bi-plane flying over the sand dunes, the stories around the glimmering campfire, the paintings of swimmers in the caves. The mating of camels, however, did not have quite the romance of nights by the campfire beneath the desert stars.

A GUIDE TO THE CINEMA

Three kinds of film used to be commonly shown in the public cinemas of Sudan: Kung Fu, Egyptian and Indian. If you asked someone what was on in the cinema, no one would know the title of the film; it was just the genre that mattered. It was just like being a *khawaja* in Sudan: *khawajas* ('white' foreigners) are often not addressed by name, for that would be to see you as an individual, but are regularly addressed with the generic *ya khawaja*. Indeed it could be said that some Sudanese have a *khawaja* complex; you might be put on a pedestal, or you might occasionally be addressed with the contempt reserved for the *kuffar*, the unbelievers.

When I was still new and green in Sudan, someone in the street asked if I was a Muslim. I said I wasn't. And then he asked if I was a Christian, and – I don't think he meant in the broad cultural sense of the word

– I said I wasn't. With this he rose to his full authority, for he was a man of some stature, and addressed the crowd who had gathered in the street.

'You're a communist!' I was in Atbara, the centre of the railways and communism in Sudan, and in those days there were still railways that ran and more than a sprinkling of communists. His was a simple reasoning: if you weren't a practising Christian or Muslim, then the only other option open to you was Communism.

It followed the same pattern as the cinema, with the three genres of films that used to be screened, as the audience ate their sunflower seeds in the open air and spat the husks on to the cement floor. There is hardly a cinema now left in the country, although I hear there is one in the ghastly Afra Mall. If you were not the first kind of believer, nor categorized as one of the 'people of the book', you just had to be the third.

It's tempting to compare the politics to the climate. When you step off the plane, even at night, it's like every hairdryer in the world is being turned on your face. In Khartoum for all but the brief winter, the heat is intense, building up until it might rain in July, the overcast sky like a lid keeping in the heat, as in a saucepan. Those clouds might herald rain, or maybe the sky would just turn a murky yellow and the land darken as the *haboub* crossed from the desert and blanketed the city, the gusts of wind carrying the dust into every nook and cranny of your home. Maybe Khartoum would be blessed with rain – it happens a few times each year – and an hour or two later, such is the intensity of the downpour, and the wealth of plastic bags blocking the drains, you would be wading through the streets as homes in the shanty towns collapsed.

Are the politics as extreme as the climate? Before my time in Sudan, President Numeiri moved from a leftist ideology to share power with Islamists; anything to stay in power. A milestone in the history of Sudan was when Numeiri – and some Sudanese never tire of telling you this – showed his apparent commitment to *sharia* by dumping supplies of alcohol in the Nile, although he himself knew his Scotch. It went far beyond alcohol however; dissidents were executed.

Sudan is not a place of gradually changing scenery. Viewing the landscapes of the Sudan from his plane, Kapuscinski savoured the deep ochre shades of the Sahara bordered by the emerald fields by the Nile and concluded that in such landscapes there were no intermediate shades or gradations.[21]

Indeed, as I flew west one early morning from Khartoum, I saw it like that: first there was brown Omdurman, with surprisingly straight squares of flat-roofed homes with their yards and mud walls, almost uniformly drab, its outskirts fading into the monotones of parched uncultivated land. Then there was the shock of irrigated fields, tenderly green, and then, sharply defined in the morning light, the Blue Nile, delighting in its own unhurried bending, turning back on itself, meandering, pleasuring in its own existence, like some sentence of languid prose.

Perhaps the phrase 'there are no intermediate shades here' applies not only to the physical geography. You could see it in the wealth. I would visit an expat friend in the flat he had rented that was spacious enough for a football game; in the entrance to the block the gaffer and his wife, refugees from Eritrea, lived in a space under the stairs.

And then there was the rural-urban divide. There was Khartoum, and maybe the Gezira, and then there was everywhere else. I would move between Khartoum with its elegant glass towers redefining the skyline as some aspired to make Khartoum a new Dubai, and the likes of Blue Nile State, where for many a village child education did not much go beyond attending the traditional school, the *khalwa*, to recite the Quran. Villagers living in mud huts by the main road still got their water from a roadside pump and would be lucky to have electricity.

In Blue Nile State a carpenter in the *suq* invited me home for coffee. We sat in the pleasant yard with its traditional grass fencing in a neighbourhood of thatched huts, his father putting the creases in the younger son's police uniform with a charcoal iron as we chatted. I admired their traditional home, which had some rooms of brick and some with the traditional thatch and mud walls. This was in the town, a town that appeared to me basically unchanged from the days of British rule, such had been the utter lack of development, apart from the spread of mobile phones and plastic chairs. I once witnessed a Falata pastoralist with a bow and quiver of arrows get a top-up for his mobile phone in the *suq*.

Many of the villages of Blue Nile State are an untidy scattering of thatched huts beneath bare baobabs. The lad was having none of what I found picturesque.

'What do they think we are, living with all this thatch? Chickens?' And when I asked who his officer was, he just replied,

'One of those Arabs!' Exasperated by what he saw as his lack of a future in Sudan, he spoke, like thousands and thousands of others, of his need to emigrate, but his description of Sudan was to me extraordinary.

'*Sudan daieg! Sudan daieg!!!!*' Sudan, a country at that time of almost a million square miles, was for him

At the *khalwa*, Ganees, Blue Nile State

Village between Damazine and Rosseires, Blue Nile State

a tight, confining place. I had to laugh! But then I wasn't a young man, not yet 20, on a salary of about US$100 a month.

And then there is the issue of the law. The law in Sudan, to a westerner, might appear as extreme as the gap between the rich and the poor. However, in *sharia* law there are some safeguards: there must be at least four witnesses in the case of accusations of adultery, eight if the witnesses are all women, for a woman's witness is worth half of a man's, with each witness having to see the 'brush' go into the 'bottle'. With such provisions, an accusation of adultery is unlikely under *sharia* law. But in Sudan a man being found alone in a room with a woman to whom he was not related could be taken as evidence of the intention to have intercourse and they could be charged.

Which brings me to a Sudanese joke. Adarawb – we shall meet this tribesman of the east later – was discovered drunk one day and the policeman swore that if he ever caught Adarawb intoxicated again he would be punished. Some days later, the policeman caught him in the street with the plastic container for carrying the alcohol.

'I've got you this time!' he said, and took him to the police station.

'But I haven't drunk anything!'

'Yes, but you have the container – this proves you had the intention to drink!' Adarawb pointed down to his crotch.

'And does the possession of this equipment also make me guilty of adultery?'

A Sudanese, in my experience, is either absolutely teetotal or he knocks it back and, given the days of Camel Beer are gone, the usual drink is *araquay*: the spirit distilled from dates that is said to be so pure it will evaporate before it touches the ground if you pour it – something I have never seen happen, of course, and the wasted state of the regular drinkers points to anything but purity. The local *araquay* is not something to be sipped and savoured; the master of ceremonies pours a glass from the bottle and you knock it back in one go and grimace. He then pours the next man the next glass, and so the single glass goes round the drinkers, back and forth, until the bottle is empty. If a Sudanese drinks, he drinks!

Are people's political views also extreme? Certain events in Khartoum, such as the groups calling for the death of an English teacher in the unfortunate 'teddy bear incident', do suggest to the world a place of intense political feeling. Ironically, the relevant law in this case was based on a blasphemy law from when the British ruled Sudan.[22]

It could even descend into farce, as when Lubna al-Hussein was prosecuted for wearing trousers (she sent out invitations to her trial) even though the uniform for females in the police service is a tunic worn over trousers, and the air hostesses on the national airline wear trousers. There has been a deliberate cultivation of drabness among women, something very much against the lovely pastels of the traditional Sudanese *tobes*: it could be called an imported dowdiness.

Events as far away as Scandinavia could fire emotions in Khartoum. Once when I went out to buy a few groceries at the local shop, a customer confronted me in English for my lack of respect. The ignorant tend to speak English; those without any English, like the lads who ran the shop, are usually courtesy itself. I looked down to check I was not offending public morality – I would never want to do that! – but I was properly dressed. But then I realised there was an offending object in my hand: a tin of condensed milk bought in another grocer's across the way. I had unknowingly bought something Danish, and emotions were still running high in 2006 after the cartoons in a Danish newspaper.

Are extreme views a response to western interference in the internal affairs of the Arabic-speaking world? Looking back on such events I can see the explorer Thesiger's view of westernization: he saw something

Grocer in Malakal

indigenous – an age-old moral code perhaps – being destroyed by the adoption of something half-baked and alien. But Thesiger did rather tend towards the view of education expressed by Oscar Wilde's Lady Bracknell, who compared 'ignorance' to a delicate exotic fruit that would lose its bloom if touched by education. Ironically, Thesiger himself, as he mapped those almost untravelled landscapes in the Empty Quarter of Arabia, was actually a herald of the modern world with its cars and oil refineries, participating in the destruction of what he loved.

I would be conscious of maybe doing something similar as an English teacher, whether it was on a Yemeni island or in Rumbek in the Dinka lands of South Sudan. I was in a sense working on the frontier between the indigenous and the global, participating in the inexorable spread of the English language and the McCulture that is enshrined in the course books with their US icons and vacant celebrities and burgers to the detriment of what is indigenous and diverse.

This loss of diversity in culture went beyond language to dress, with the men of the professional classes abandoning their white *jelabiyahs* and generous *immas* (over a metre of cloth might be dexterously wrapped about the head) for some shiny suit. Ironically, it was mainly during the years of Islamization and Arabization that indigenous dress styles were lost.

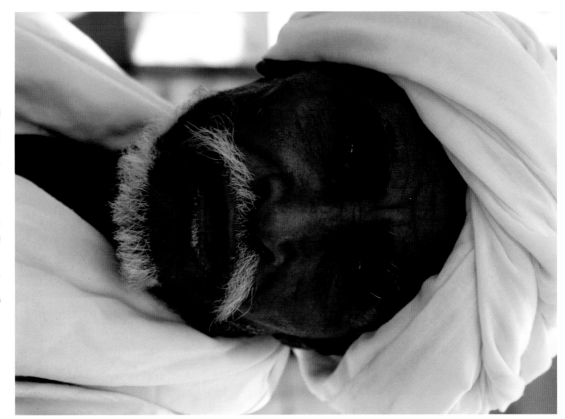

Traditional elegance in Damazine Suq

Ma fi are two of the first words you learn in Sudan: 'There isn't any!' It seems to me that the Sudanese take a great delight in these two words. I once ordered a banana split in an ice-cream parlour in downtown Khartoum, only to find it arrive without a banana. Without irony the server just called out as he served up my banana-free banana split:

'*Mozz ma fi!*' Yes, we have no bananas!

Even officials can be decent sometimes. Once I ended up trying to get an exit visa at about 3.00 pm – the equivalent at home would be turning up in an office at 4.55 pm on a Friday and expecting someone to assist you. In the deserted office I asked the officer responsible, handsomely uniformed and moustached, if there was any chance of an exit visa, as there was a flight to Egypt the next day. He picked up my passport then turned in his droll way to his partner.

'We've nothing against the Irish, have we?' The desired stamp came down. The only problem now was that having felt sure that I would not get an exit visa, I had cancelled my booking for the flight.

It can be a bit frustrating, dealing with it all. Unlike, say, in Yemen, where there is an unwritten rule that westerners can take in a couple of bottles with them in their hand luggage – after all, if they are not Muslims why shouldn't they? – in Sudan it's a different

Despite incidents like those just mentioned, I'm not going to draw a parallel between environmental extremes and extremist views. In daily life, as I have encountered them in Khartoum, the Sudanese show not extremism but moderation and tolerance. They exhibit a humour about events around them, keep their heads down a bit and are not much fooled by officialdom. They can see through it all, especially now when everything is so jaded.

Another approach is the ostrich position: they just deny that certain things – well known to foreigners perhaps – are happening. And for the ostriches in Sudan, there's no shortage of sand. In addition, those without satellite TV get a very limited view of events from the state media. Indeed there's a phrase, 'newspaper talk', for something that is obviously a fabrication. Apart from football, which is the national obsession, there's not a lot of information available. I discovered this officially when, doing a tour of the sites near Karima, I popped into a local office of the Ministry of Information. The civil servant sitting at her desk welcomed me warmly, adjusting her *tobe* to make sure everything was correct. After I had repeated my request for information, she laughed, and called out with delight in her blend of English and Arabic:

'Information? Information *ma fi*! There isn't any information!'

matter. Perhaps because Sudan is on the periphery the authorities feel the need to be more extreme. Before a flight from Damascus to Khartoum, I agonized about whether or not to smuggle anything in. Arriving in the early hours of the morning, nicely tanked up but with nothing in the luggage, it was somewhat exasperating to have the taxi driver at the airport pass over his cup and invite me to partake of the local spirit.

In his novel *Season of Migration to the North*, the Sudanese novelist Tayeb Salih portrays life in the backwater of a northern village situated in a bend in the Nile. There the villagers attend the mosque, till the fields, do their prayers, knock back the *araquay* and enjoy a bawdy banter. As they down the local poison, Bint Majzoub tells the assembled men of the pleasure one of her late husbands had given her from the evening call to prayer right through until dawn. One thing the Sudanese are not, despite all that is imposed by the authorities, is puritanical.

In the novel, the narrator returns to Sudan and is asked about life abroad. Europe in the popular imagination is a place where children have to leave home on their sixteenth birthday and everyone enjoys sex without marrying. The narrator, however, says that he found people abroad just like the Sudanese, in that they married and brought up their children according to principles and traditions. They were generally good people.[23]

Rather than falling for comparisons to extreme landscapes and extreme climates, I feel I should return the compliment. When it comes to religion, I'd say the Muslim Sudanese, as I have known them, tend to be genuine and a bit pragmatic. There are many who are devout and teetotal, and there are some who live decent lives and do their evening prayers and then open the bottle, in private, for it's Thursday night. And no matter what might be said by some clerics, certain officials excepted, they will almost certainly deal with a westerner with that lovely Sudanese combination of decency and humour.

Who could not find the Sudanese attractive, with those looks and that affability, not to mention their laughter? And when I think of the men who gather around the tea-ladies in my street, who would not warm to their good natures, and spontaneity, and their irreverent sense of humour? And who could not forgive them those little vices they have; their garrulous nature, perhaps, or their contempt for western concepts of punctuality, or their addiction to yet another spoonful of sugar in the tea?

Which brings me to the crunch. The Sudanese themselves never tire of telling you what lovely people they are. I don't know any other people who do this, who say to you, 'We are lovely people, *naas taibeen*,' and wait

Last days of the pontoon, Atbara

for you to confirm it. And who could argue with that? To me, they are the salt of the earth. But how can it be – and here comes the question that after all those years in Sudan I struggle to ask, let alone answer – how can it be that among such lovely people, such heinous crimes have been committed, Sudanese against Sudanese?

TITANIC

Before I returned to Sudan yet again I was doing a stint in the wilds of Yemen, among the tribesmen of Mareb. My students would leave their Kalashnikovs against the wall inside the classroom door, and the lesson would begin. Despite the array of weaponry, those sons of Mareb sheikhs were, perhaps, the most well-mannered group I have ever taught.

Work was over by 1.00 pm, and everyone went off to chew *qat*, the national weed. I, however, was confined to my hotel in case of kidnapping, unable to leave except with an armed guard. In the evenings, I was entertained in the desolate dining room with two cassettes: an Arab mix and a Celine Dion cassette featuring *Titanic*. I grew to like the Arab mix.

This kind of life was not what I had signed up for, and on my mobile, by the empty pool, I arranged a new posting as a trainer in Khartoum, with a well-known

Portrait on the day of the Camel Market, Ed Dammar

British institution. Back in Africa, far from the Sabean Temple of the Moon and the 'Throne of Bilquis', I found that some things remained unchanged: as I did my solitary lengths of the pool at the Grand, the theme tune of *Titanic* would sound out over the waters.

Had the *Titanic* theme song become the unofficial national anthem of the Arabic-speaking world? From Yemen to Khartoum, did they all feel they were on a sinking boat, doomed to be thwarted in love and other dreams? And then there was the trusty captain at the helm, who, in the Arabic version of the film, would prefer the ship to sink than hand over power to another. As the Sudanese watched events in the Arab Spring on their TVs, I would remember what they say about Khartoum, with its two seasons, one sunny and warm, the other sunny and intensely hot, 'We have no spring here!'

Even in work there was no escape. Exam candidates, asked to describe their favourite film, would inevitably talk about *Titanic*. A thousand times the Sudanese told me the Titanic sank. Exasperated, I once asked why everyone chose this one film.

'We like this film because we have no romance in our lives!' Saying this, they were echoing a Victorian Englishman's assessment of marriage among the Sudanese. In his usual candid way Samuel Baker, perhaps forgetting that he had bought his own wife Florence in a slave market and married her some years later, wrote, 'Everything is practical, without a particle of romance'.[24] Despite the unpropitious beginnings I wouldn't say that the Bakers' life together was without romance – they explored Sudan through thick and thin as a couple – and I don't think that the Sudanese are without romance either. Like Victorian England however, Khartoum is a place where it has been the norm for families to find a suitable partner for their offspring.

WEDDINGS

When you visited a village in the Gezira, you'd be introduced to the neighbours. They'd be sitting in the warmth of the evening, watching TV in the yard, and the women would stand up and adjust their *tobes* and welcome you warmly.

'This is my sister-in-law, Fatima, and my aunt on my mother's side, Jamila, and my cousin on my mother's side, Aziza.'

That was really all there was to do socially in Sudan; apart from the diversion of drinking tea under the tree, you visited your relatives. I had this confirmed in class one day.

'What is the main social activity in Sudan?' I asked.

'We visit our relative.' A feature of Sudanese English is the nationwide resistance to adding an 's' to a word to make it plural. I was not exactly overcome with curiosity.

'And what is the second most popular social activity?'

'We visit our relative in hospital.' Anyone seriously ill, who has the means or the contacts, will fly to Cairo for treatment, but for others it is a different story. Visiting relatives is an absolute necessity, for it is the relatives who will feed the patient, sometimes camping out on the pavement at night.

Family life is very much alive in Sudan: there is commitment to the family, whether it is paying school fees or hospital fees, or personal support and care for the elderly in the home. Such is the network of support from the extended family, I was told, there is at least one hospital which requires visitors to buy a ticket to enter the building. And most definitely in Sudan, even in the capital, there is a very strong sense of community, without the isolation that typifies city life in the west. You would, however, see the destitute begging in the streets. For that too my trainees had an answer, saying, 'They're foreigners.' And the same would be said of the street kids, 'They're not Sudanese!'

Scene on Tuti Island

After coffee, you'd be taken to another house and meet another set of relatives, for it seems sometimes in the villages that everyone is related. Given the cost of marriage, the Sudanese often marry their relatives and the wealth stays in the family. Marriage in Sudan is not generally perceived as it is in the west – a matter of two people 'falling in love' and forming a bond on that basis, a bond that often ends in divorce – but of marriage within the extended family or clan. Although this is changing now with mobile phone culture and the opportunities that the university campus allows, a young man has typically married his cousin. And it is not the bride herself who signs the contract – after all, she is a woman – a male guardian will do that on her behalf.

Traditionally, in order to marry, apart from the money aspect of the dowry itself, a Sudanese man has to supply seven *tobes* and seven pairs of shoes and all the other sevens that make up the *sheilah* or trousseau. But if he is marrying a relative, the wealth stays within the family circle. And so the proverb: *Zeitna fi beitna* – my oil stays in my house. *Zeit* literally means 'oil', for example, cooking oil. A very free translation would be that our wealth stays in our family when we marry our own.

I am thinking here of those Sudanese I know best: the 'Arab' Muslims. For me in Khartoum, weddings among the middle-class were occasions for gross conspicuous consumption, but then that is not unique to the Sudanese. Weddings were the main event in the social calendar.

'Have you been to a Sudanese wedding?' acquaintances would ask with enthusiasm, and I would inwardly groan at the idea. This, however, was not quite as tiresome as another set invitation, one that, of course, brought with it conditions, usually by a man who was himself single.

'We'll give you a Sudanese woman to marry!' Or, within the context of marriage:

'How much does a woman cost in your country?'

A good insight into another aspect of sexual relations was in Wau in the South of Sudan, where I used to frequent an open-air bar near the river. One night, I drank with one of my trainees, a massive guy, one of the biggest Sudanese I have ever met, who had fought with the Sudan People's Liberation Army (SPLA) but was now one of the Joint Units, a force forged from both Khartoum's Sudan Armed Forces (SAF) and the SPLA to uphold the Comprehensive Peace Agreement of 2005. As some band from Zaire sounded out in all its joyful excess from the sound system, and an attractive Ugandan waitress set another couple of beers on the table, that guerrilla fighter's hand, out of the blue, rested firmly on my thigh. He turned to me and confessed rather intimately, 'In our culture it is not possible for one man to love another'. It was, looking back on it, what I like to think of as one of those Sudanese moments. 'Instead, a man gives him his daughter to marry.'

That trainee had broken a taboo. I think he was being honest in portraying relations among the same gender as something beyond the norms of their culture. The men of the North, however, are different and may enjoy the banter of innuendo, and what I might call an ambiguous flirtation, not to mention the citizens of that city of the plain, Medani, once railed at by Numeiri for their 'immorality'.25 It's there in the ambiguities of the language; it's hardly remarkable for one man to address another, often in a slightly tongue in cheek way, as 'delicious' or 'handsome' or 'honey', although referring to an attractive youth as a *sammak* – meaning fish – does lose something in translation.

For the Sudanese, a wedding may be a rare chance to dance with the other sex. But the extremists would frown even on dancing at weddings, and more often than not the 'party' would be just groups seated at tables consuming a soft drink. Alcohol would not be on offer, but I'm sure some of the *shebab* would get tanked up first.

The last wedding I went to was with my colleagues in one of those halls by the airport where we dutifully sat at our tables and waited for the bride and groom to arrive, watching it all on the big screens. The bride had endured the period of confinement, the *habis* (it is the word used to refer to gaol), that comes before the wedding, when she is not to leave the house, for she is being fattened up for the events ahead, and also the sun might darken her complexion. You can see the grooms, as well, in the barber's, getting their skin lightened with a cream, the face a ghoulish mask of white. A few months later, having performed his primary duty, the groom left for Pakistan.

A wedding up in Shendi might offer a little more diversion. It is well known that among the Ja'aliyyin the groom will take the leather whip he has for the occasion and his most intimate friends will remove their shirts and vests for the lash to come down on their backs. When his friends get married, they return the compliment, with a lash or two thrown in for good measure. At least it is not the traditional Dinka whip made from a bull's penis.

I've never witnessed this proof of manhood at a wedding (what is Sudanese society if not a celebration of maleness, and a somewhat conventional maleness at that?) but in a village near Atbara, I did see it at a baby's naming ceremony, after the wife of a friend of mine had given birth to a son. Jamal had that wild untamed spirit of youth when I knew him first, with a mass of uncombed hair and, although settled in a village by the

Jamal at home, near Atbara

banks of the Nile, he was somehow bedouin in his spirit. After his wife's required time of 40 days' rest, the birth could be celebrated. In the evening, the entertainment began. Jamal stripped to the waist, and his cousin brought his whip down maybe half a dozen times on his back, as Jamal leaned on his stick, one leg raised above the ground, like some dandy hoping to win the admiration of the crowd. Then the other male guests took their turn.

The next morning, the men were not feeling quite so macho, saying it was too cold to swim in the Nile. But after breakfast they assembled for another round, the whip coming down on already marked flesh, which must have made the morning after considerably more memorable than the night before.

HOSPITALITY

One of the pleasures of being in Sudan was to escape the capital and travel north, where in the towns by the Nile a more traditional way of living could be savoured. Beyond Dongola were the Mahas lands, where I could slum it in the *laconda* and hang out in the barber's and explore some lush island of the Nile.

This was the land of ancient Nubia, with many still speaking the Nubian language as their mother tongue. And the museum at Kerma Deffufa, its very name

referring to the royal mound of the site, celebrates Kushite culture. Arriving around midday, I found it closed for the early afternoon.

To fill the vacuum until the museum re-opened, I walked down a track where I was invited to join a group just setting about slaughtering a sheep. That was my first invitation. And then by the palms, one of the lads tending the plantations asked me back home. That was my second invitation. All the family were away, and given there were no women to make tea he offered me a cup of water. He himself found a small bag of snuff tucked under a mattress or somewhere, the 'tobacco' that some Sudanese stick under their lower lip as a stimulant. It's not the most attractive of habits, and I asked:

'So you take that stuff?' I was surprised by this young villager's ennui.

'What else is there to do?'

I continued my walk among palm plantations but a car stopped. The driver and his wife invited me to join them for lunch. I politely refused this, the third invitation. They insisted and I got in. The main room of their home was not unpleasing to the eye with just beds and a couple of tables for furniture. My host's lifestyle was not unenviable. For about eight months of the year he worked in Saudi Arabia and returned to the farm for the remainder of the year.

My hosts, Kerma Deffufa

After lunch, with just the men eating together, my host drove me back to the museum as promised. On the way we passed one of those conical clay domes that are built outside the houses.

'Is it for pigeons?' There was another of those Sudanese moments as the host turned to his passenger and confessed.

'Pigeon meat is a great aphrodisiac!'

I did my dutiful tour of the museum, which, to its credit was full of local people enjoying a day out. I gazed at the monumental statues of the rulers of the Nubian dynasty carved in black granite from the times when Kerma had been the centre of the Kingdom of Kush, statues that had been ritually broken and buried in a pit, only to be restored and now exhibited in the gallery. The other exhibits were not just the delicate clay pots of the ancient past, but also items from recent rural life: skirts that girls used to wear, the wooden boards that are still written on with charcoal in the Quranic schools, kitchen utensils before blenders arrived.

I had met one of the labourers who had helped build the museum by the banks of the Nile in Dongola, below the yellow flowers of the acacia trees, heavy with pollen. Ibrahim was standing by an old boat, washing his clothes with Tide, hunched on his hunkers behind a basin. We swam, and then he soaped himself down with the washing powder too. Ibrahim was pure Nuban. He had invited me back to sip tea beneath the palms outside the walls of his sister's family home. I had asked him about his accommodation during the year he had spent building the museum.

'We slept on the ground.' And the food?

'We cooked for ourselves.' And in Ramadan?

'I fasted and worked.' And pay?

'At that time it was 35 Sudanese pounds a day.' At today's rates, that was about £6 sterling.

When it comes to culture, I am not one of those who love museums and historical sites, although it was clear that Kerma was not some annexe to things Egyptian, but a centre of Nubian culture with its temple and burial cult of the king. Remarkable though the museum exhibits may be, culture for me was more about the invitation to lunch: it's that simple lunch of pancake and home-grown lady's fingers, the hosts and the guest dipping into the dishes together, that I'll remember as something essentially Sudanese.

ANOTHER SOCIAL ACTIVITY

There's another tradition not uncommon among some Sudanese. To describe it, I'll turn to Kapuscinski,

who in 1960 stayed in the Grand Hotel, where Louis Armstrong was a fellow guest. Armstrong's concert in the stadium didn't go down too well; the audience didn't so much as clap. That hasn't much changed today. I once sat through a Christmas event at one of Khartoum's international hotels, with Ethiopian women dancing in Santa Claus outfits. Given the response of the audience, they might as well have held the event in a morgue.

In the restaurant near work, I would mock the entertainment on Sudanese television as workers partook of their *fuul* beans or a pancake with a savoury sauce. Two brothers ran the place, directing the Ethiopians or Eritreans serving up the fried liver. With their wonderfully self-deprecating sense of humour I could gently mock the society that they both loved and endured. On the screen there would be images of the Sudanese having a good time: groups seated around plastic tables, the women unsmiling, and with nothing on the table, least of all a drink.

'What's that, by God, we're watching today?' 'What's that on?' I'd call to the diners scooping up their *fuul* beans on a piece of bread.

'Now is that a wedding or a funeral you're watching?'

A colleague once described Khartoum as 'austere'. We were sitting in an embassy bar at the time, with the

security lights shining directly down on our heads. I objected, of course, for I've never laughed more than with the Sudanese, but I could see his point. However, I see the door self-righteousness that exists at times as something imposed from above, something even imported, perhaps, whether from the Muslim Brothers in Egypt or the Salafi version of Islam in Saudi Arabia, and used as a means of political control, rather than as something genuinely Sudanese.

But Kapuscinski's short stay in Khartoum was a memorable one. A couple of men he assumed to be university students approached him, and they drove off into the desert where they had a great view of the Nile. And then, as night fell, Kapuscinski shared a not uncommon aspect of Sudanese hospitality.

That evening, the Nile glimmered with silver light, for it was illuminated by the desert moon. His companions offered him a drink and they also shared something that is grown in parts of Sudan. All was calm and quiet on that escarpment above the Nile.

For Kapuscinski the desert landscape took on qualities that hint of a Van Gogh painting. He seemed to rise up from the ground among multi-coloured circles and float through dark but luminous skies.[26] The next morning he woke with a terrible headache.

CONDOLENCES

Another social occasion would be funerals, when the street would be cordoned off and the mourners would gather over coffee. They were also a good opportunity to skip work; the entire workplace would disappear to offer condolences if the boss's cousin died back in the village.

In Omdurman there's a street of tailors where I used to go after classes. As the merchants of the *suq* shut up their shops and the Singer machines hummed, I'd sip tea with the tailors who were nearly all from the South. I'd have to avoid the tanner who'd press me to have a glass of tea, and shake hands with the length of the street, interrupting the tailors as they put the final touches to a soldier's uniform or cut the cloth of a civilian's polyester trousers.

When the son of one of the tailors died, I went with some of his mates to offer condolences. His house was somewhere like New Omdurman, where water was brought by barrel and donkey, and lighting was a wick in a can. I had expected the set mourning of the Muslim Sudanese, with the canopy covering the street and the crowd of mourners sipping coffee in the shade. But we were some days late, and there was no one except his wife, so we said a few words and left for a drink.

We didn't have far to go; one of the neighbouring houses had a still and they kindly showed me the workings of it. Someone ordered a bottle and we passed around the glass, throwing back the contents in one go, for *araquay* is not something you would want to savour, and left the house feeling quite merry.

And there in the street was George. We offered our condolences in a sheepish kind of way, embarrassed at our own enjoyment on such an occasion, and he walked us down to the bus stop. We went back in the bus in silence, our mouths tightly shut so that no one might smell our breath.

Years later, I again went to offer my condolences, this time on the outskirts of Khartoum. Near my flat there were lads from Darfur who offered a valet service in the street, outside the chemist's advertising 'Fair and Lovely', the skin-lightening cream. It was a strange life they led: never getting in a car except to clean it; sending money back to the parents in Darfur; renting a room in areas like Salvation and Mayo and Mandela; talking of the streams and orange groves of Jebbel Mirrah.

One day, I heard that the son of one of the Darfur lads, aged about six months, had passed away. So we did the Sudanese thing and, after his mates had changed out of their overalls, went to pay our condolences. The home

Tailor, Omdurman Suq

was out beyond the outskirts, with some of the houses still surrounded by the earth that had been put down to try and stop them being washed away in the last rains.

They said the *al-fatiha*, reciting the opening words of the Quran as required, as I held up my hands in supplication, and then talked pleasantries. We then listened to how the infant had developed a fever, so that I wondered about the wisdom of drinking the glass of water proffered by the host, for the water is brought in a barrel by donkeys. It was interesting to contrast the realities of their lives with what I had been told by a significantly bearded candidate answering a set question in an exam.

'And do all the homes in your city have clean water?'

'Oh yes.'

'Even the homes on the outskirts?'

'Oh yes. They all have piped water.'

'So what then are those donkeys doing, bringing water in barrels to the homes?'

'Ah! Those people! Those people don't like the taste of the piped water so they have water brought privately!'

CHECKING INTO A *LACONDA* IN SOUTH KORDOFAN

A *laconda* is something downmarket from a hotel, but the *laconda* in Umm Ruwaba was not unpleasant, and neither was the manager. The *suq* here was sheltered with lovely *dom* palms that give it a certain grace and the vegetable market was a mountain of water melons.

The *laconda* was home to lads from al Gezira trading in this and that, and the manager, with bearded vigour and *sirwal* trousers above the ankles, ran the place well. For 4 Sudanese pounds I got a mattress and a clean sheet.

The yard was wonderfully spacious with maybe 20 beds, but with the cool nights of winter most guests chose to sleep inside. I was looking forward to sleeping outside at last under the moon and the stars; in the morning I would wake to the kites that nest in the trees in the yard flying overhead.

But before I could book in, the manager told me I had to register with 'Security'. This involved a walk through the residential areas, with their external walls hiding the yards and rooms of Sudanese domesticity. Near a police station, kids lined against a wall were incredibly irritating with their cat-calls, and as the sun set I vented my annoyance on two men who looked as if they were in public service.

'Obviously there's not a lot of schooling going on in this place!'

'The *shamasha* are a problem...'

'They don't much look like street kids to me. And I have to go and report to "Security" here in order to sleep for a night in the *laconda*!'

Guest in the *laconda*

'It's for your benefit!' That's one of my favourite lines anywhere: 'It's for your safety.'

At dusk I reached the 'Security' office. This is where Sudanese hospitality falls a little short; unlike the grassroots Sudanese who will insist on buying the traveller tea, in such an office you'll not be offered a glass of water. Those who govern have forgotten what it is to be Sudanese.

I took in the aesthetics: the main feature of the room was the bare desk, on which there was neither a computer nor a sheet of paper. It's all fairly minimalistic in a Sudanese office. There might be a newspaper however, for, as Lady Bracknell said about smoking, 'a man should have an occupation'.

The props of this government office were a copy of the Quran on the desk, and a bed. That's how it is. The TV was turned to Fox Movies of course; the Saudi channel is not quite so popular. Was I the only one to see the dichotomy between the holy book on the table and the 24-hour diet of Hollywood movies?

I handed over my passport and explained.

'I'm a teacher working in Khartoum. This is my week's holiday between Christmas and the New Year.' Christmas dinner this year would be at a table in the market. Obviously my Arabic was incomprehensible, for the official asked again what I did in Khartoum.

Venue for my Christmas lunch, al-Rashad

'I'm an English teacher. This is my week's holiday between Christmas and the New Year.'

I left him to delve into the mysteries of my passport, which has raised a few eyebrows at Heathrow: Sudan, Yemen, Syria, Lebanon. I stood watching the Fox film, a thriller set in what I took to be 1960s America that involved black youths and the kidnapping of a white woman. As my plain-clothes police officer went through my documentation, the Hollywood detective

CONVERSATION WITH AN *AMJAD* DRIVER

There was a whole bush telegraph network in Khartoum, and I would get my news not from the media, but from those I chatted to in the taxis or over a glass of tea in the street.

Basically, in Khartoum, apart from the dire bus service, you can take a variety of transport which has its own hierarchy. First are the taxis, old men driving old yellow vehicles. Then there are the *amjads*, small minibuses that function as taxis and allow intimate conversations with the driver, who is often a graduate in engineering or the like who has found no alternative employment.

The third option is a rickshaw, the most downmarket form of transport, and the most delightful, usually driven by one of the *shebab* who may have ended up doing an arts degree. In terms of engine power, the nearest thing to a rickshaw in the west is a lawnmower, but with three wheels. The drivers are a subculture in Sudan, with their own slang. To know the rickshaw drivers is to know urban Sudan.

One evening after a pizza in the Grand, I eventually managed to wave down an *amjad*. The driver had a handsome face, a shaven head, and a white *jelabiyah*.

'Are you one of the Ja'aliyyin?' I asked, for he had the uncompromising masculinity of the males of the

stuck his gun in the mouth of one of the black suspects and pulled the trigger. It didn't go off. My enjoyment of the film was disrupted.

'Take off your cap!' The normal courtesies that are part and parcel of daily Sudanese life seem to disappear in government offices.

'When is your date of entry to Sudan?'

Should I say 1986? Back on the screen, the New York cops had surrounded the kidnappers' home. The detective went in first, alone. And now my passport was ignored as the suspense of the scene captured both traveller and official. The hostage taker, black, was sitting alone in his underwear, watching TV. The detective, white, entered the room and shot him dead. He placed a gun in the hand of the corpse, and then went to comfort the hostage.

My cop melted slightly:

'Is that how it is over there?' I didn't ask him how it was in Kordofan.

As I left, he expressed his desire for English lessons, but I would not be queuing up for that one. I could now go to the *laconda*. The full moon would bathe me in its light as I slept with all my clothes on and an ample supply of insect repellent to keep mosquitoes at bay.

But just as I walked past the police station, one of the men standing there called me over.

'Where are you from?' Oh no, not again...

Ja'aliyyin tribe who dominate Sudan. The Sudanese are not ones for pretensions.

'Me? I'm from Tuti Island. I'm a peasant! Just now I've been picking lemons in the orchard.'

Tuti Island is one of my favourite places in Khartoum, an island on the Blue Nile with lemon groves and onion fields and streets just wide enough for one donkey to pass another. The islanders are a conservative people, and for a long time rejected plans to build a bridge to link their island to Khartoum. And so they would wait in the shade of the mahogany trees on Nile Avenue for the ferry that went back and forth every quarter of an hour or so. Even on the wide ferry there was segregation of the sexes in those days of Salvation, with the men in their *jelabiyahs* standing on one side of the metal vessel and the women in their splendid *tobes* standing on the other.

I would often take the ferry over to walk through the irrigated fields of clover and savour the bird-life: pure white cattle egrets in the fields, fire-finches crimson among the bushes, lapwings calling to decoy the walker away from their eggs.

It was the combination of greenness and Nile waters that made the island for me, not to mention the affability of the labourers from Darfur or Shendi working in the fields. It was on Tuti Island that I was once rebuked for mocking the organisation I think of

as the Gravy Train: one of the displaced, now tilling the soil or minding livestock, said that it was because of the presence of this international peace-promoting organisation that he was alive.

Once, one of the farm workers, having invited me for tea, quoted how he felt about the island:

Greenness and water and a lovely face
Give pleasure.

And then, given that I had declined their invitation to tea outside their straw *rokuba*, his friend asked why we foreigners refused hospitality.

Rickshaw, Rosseires

But things were changing on the island. A rash of building was taking place, as the driver explained.

'It's not like before; they've sold the land to one side of me and also to the other, so there's hardly anywhere left to farm.' I also felt that the island was losing its charm; instead of taking the ferry as before, anyone could now just drive across.

'That bridge the Chinese built is a disaster for the island!' Soon, green Tuti would be just another nondescript area of Khartoum, its drabness highlighted by the Blue Nile that defines it.

We passed through the usual deserted urban landscapes, but that night the city centre seemed to be particularly dreary. Downtown Khartoum sometimes has the feel of a city that has come through some cataclysm: there are buildings with their concrete skeleton structures intact, but without walls, the project incomplete for years, as if the investor had run out of money, or interest. At night, occasional street-lamps spill pools of light onto the pavements, deserted except for the crowds milling around outside the hospitals.

Another detail of the Khartoum landscape is the little piles of reddish mud bricks stacked here and there, heaped up against a wall or arranged to form a pile on the pavement, near where the desert sand gathers in drifts against the kerb or a wall, little monuments

Tuti Islander

to incompletion, unfulfilled bricks that have never actually got to be part of a building, maybe tomorrow, *inshallah*. But they have their uses: where the tea-ladies have packed up their paraphernalia to go home, you can see a rough semi-circle of bricks that were make-shift seats.

The driver explained.

'They're all asleep; sleeping away the first day of Ramadan.'

'Well, I hope you managed to 'poke the coals', if you know what I mean, before you started Ramadan! I know it's the kind of thing you guys do!' And indeed, some of the lads do things deemed not quite *halal* in the final days before Ramadan. He laughed again.

'Your Arabic is one hundred per cent!'

'I've lived in Damascus.'

'And how is Khartoum?'

'Paradise!' He looked at me, not at first getting the irony, although of all the countries where I could live in the region, to live among the Sudanese would be my first choice, for where else is so culturally rich? And who can match the Sudanese for their good looks and charm, yet be so unaware of how attractive they are?

Ramadan in Khartoum is not like those Arab capitals such as Sana'a and Damascus, where there is an almost festive atmosphere in the evening with shoppers and crowds milling around the buzzing streets. The Sudanese have that lovely thing of breaking the fast with their neighbours, eating shared dishes in the street, the dishes of food laid out on mats on the ground, and that is it socially, apart from the prayers.

It is not just the urban landscapes that suggest cataclysm. Travelling through the Gezira, the landscape is one of a murky sky meeting a monochrome plain, the only relief the dome of some sheikh's tomb or a dust devil soaring above the dry land. There are, however, the colours of spring: soft pinks, lemons, sky-blues, like the colours of the women's *tobes*, but these flowers are the infinite array of plastic bags blossoming in the fields and clinging to the fences and thorn bushes. Without irony, a Sudanese will turn to you and say, 'Isn't Sudan a beautiful country?'

Travelling in the hills of Kordofan, I could see what they mean. Despite all that has happened there, a way of rural life was somehow still intact when I travelled near al-Rashad, with the women leisurely walking to market with the produce from their own market gardens for sale, their path winding below baobabs and desert rose blossoming on rocky outcrops, and they would laughingly engage with the foreigner on the road. But nearer the towns, I would point to the plastic bags clinging to the thorn bushes and say, 'If plastic bags were flowers, we'd be in paradise.' The driver clicked.

Walking home, market day, to Jebbel Falata, al-Rashad, Kordofan

Encounter on the road, al-Rashad, Kordofan

'The problem's money! There's no money!' I could think of a few other issues myself, how the money from oil revenues was spent for instance, but let that one pass. The Khartoum landscape had, however, changed over the past few years with the signing of the Comprehensive Peace Agreement, and elegant buildings have transformed the skyline.

My driver turned out to be someone who had travelled.

'I've lived abroad myself, in Saudi and Libya. But your accent is easy to understand.'

'In Sudan some think my accent is Syrian. Once I was called an Iraqi traitor here!' That had been in Malakal, where, having chatted a bit in Arabic to the guys hanging out in the *suq*, I was told I was not Irish but an Iraqi traitor. Another day there, walking by the Nile, someone called out that I was an Egyptian spy. Such are the levels of paranoia among some, speaking Arabic is equated with espionage!

It's in the privacy of an *amjad* or taxi that the Sudanese open up.

'I lived in Iraq myself. I was there during the war. We tried to leave, to enter Iran but they wouldn't let Muslims in, only Shias.'

The driver's exit from Iraq had been an ordeal.

'There were four buses leaving, and I tried to board the first, but the driver wouldn't let me on – there was no room. But the driver of the next bus was Sudanese and I got on.' His had been a lucky escape.

'Over 40 Egyptians died when the bus in front was bombed from the air. You just see a flash and you are hit. And over 20 Sudanese died.'

'All civilians?'

'Civilians! There were 11 of us Sudanese living in one house; 9 died in that bus! I was the only one to return to Sudan.'

I have no way of verifying what he said; I am just recalling words after the event, from memory, or maybe from notes written some time after the conversation. So the dialogues recorded here are not just documented by me but are also partly created by me; it would be naïf to claim otherwise. And then someone might say, 'How can you speak for the Sudanese?' I might say that I am not, but I'm trying to show how we interacted, as I travelled from place to place, or as I just went about my daily life, for it's possible to live in the most exotic of places – what sounds more exotic than the Nile? – and still live a very routine life.

Alternatively, I might point to Gertrude Bell, one of the greatest of all those subversive, imperialist travellers like Richard Burton and T.E. Lawrence, who, as she travelled through Syria with her servants and china, and a volume of Persian poetry in her saddle bag, perhaps, caught the pearls of conversation that fell from the bedouin around the campfire, and strung them together in *The Desert and the Sown*.

In contrast, I would jump into an *amjad* after bargaining the fare down from 10 Sudanese pounds to 7, and after the ten minute journey between the Traffic Police Roundabout and the flat, having chatted with the driver in the intimacy of his vehicle, with his seat-belt undone but with a copy of the Quran on the dashboard to protect him from accidents, I would try and recall the gist of the conversation, and string our words together.

We had reached Khartoum Two and the driver pulled over near the police station. Officers lay stretched out in their car, the seats in full reclining position. It was, after all, Ramadan, when the entire North, at least as far as work is concerned, goes into something like a state of torpor. It is almost as if to work would be in some way to spoil the fast. There is one phrase that I don't remember ever having heard in Sudan: 'to work is to worship'.

The driver turned to me.

'You must come over to the island and break the fast with us one day, and try our Ramadan drinks.' Indeed, that is one of the most memorable times in Sudan, when you have been sitting by the Nile waiting for the sun to set – a seemingly interminable time when the Muslim Sudanese are fasting in intense heat of 40 degrees – and when the call to prayer finally sounds out, your host pours the energy-restoring drinks, made from lemons and tamarind and hibiscus.

It wasn't one of those insincere invitations that the Sudanese call 'fishermen's invitations', for fishermen, from the safe distance of their boat, are said to invite those standing on the river bank to share their food.

'What's your mobile number?' He saw me hesitate.

'Of course you mustn't worry in Sudan. It's so safe!'

People in the Arab world and in Sudan never tire of telling you how safe their country is, or at least that's what they have always said before the 'Arab Spring'. On such occasions I have had to bite my tongue and not respond by saying that a bird in a cage is also very safe, but who wants to live in a cage? And for foreigners, or those from the dominant ethnic groups i.e. those originating from communities on the banks of the Nile north of Khartoum – the Ja'aliyyin, the Shayqiyya, and the Danaqala – Khartoum is a very safe place to live.

In Khartoum, you can walk anywhere; the problem is there's nowhere to go, bar Papa Costa's for a pizza and a bit of reggae (the band still heroically sounding out after all these years) or one of those places in the new suburbs where they aspire to a Gulf lifestyle and which

I think of as the cultural desert. No matter what a few might say – their nostalgia creating a past that has never existed – I can't imagine that Khartoum ever came near to being 'the Paris of Africa'. In contrast, in Juba there are buzzing bars and cosmopolitan restaurants, but you would be unwise to set foot in the streets after dark.

My trainees from the South had a very different perspective on the 'safety' of Khartoum. One told me of the late night visits from the 'authorities' who would demand to see a couple's marriage certificate, something that might well not exist, for in some cultures it is the transfer of cattle that seals a marriage, not a legal document.

I shook hands warmly from the street through the window as I left.

'*Ramadan karem*!'

'*Allah akram*!'

RACE RELATIONS

On the eastern side of Tuti Island a little wooden sailing boat ferried passengers across the Blue Nile to Bahari, and in the winter afternoons I would go over to the shore to Bahari to bathe. The ferrymen who rowed you over were from the South, and they would always laugh at my arrival on the bank and call out.

'Where have you been, *khawaja*?' Abdullah would never call me by my name. In reply I would call down to the boat.

'And where have you been, *jenoubi*?'

For Abdullah I would give the Arabic word for Southerner the negative intonation it is usually given in Khartoum. Indeed, in the North of Sudan almost any word for another nationality seems to have a negative connotation: Ethiopian, Nigerian, Chinese, Bangladeshi… as if the Sudanese felt superior to everyone in the world. An exception was Saudi Arabia; when the grocer said something was made in Saudi, you'd think it had fallen from the heavens.

To be more precise, I could have called Abdullah *jallabi* for he is a Southern Sudanese who wears the *jelabiyah* of Muslims – *jallabi* is a common word in the South for a Northern trader. His companion, Michael, however, was Christian, and as Abdullah prayed on the shore with the islanders after sunset, Michael would sit by the boat in his shirt and trousers.

As the light faded, the last donkey would be coaxed onto the boat, and if there was no wind for the sail, someone would help Michael with the oars, and the last trip of the day was made over to Tuti, Abdullah holding out his hand for the fares as the boat touched the shore.

A SOCIAL BLUNDER

The River Atbara Hotel consisted of about 30 beds laid out in a yard and a couple of rooms where the more select guests could share a room with five strangers and maybe have a cleanish sheet on arrival. In the corner of the yard worked the dobyman, a Nuban from Kordofan, who washed the residents' clothes.

Almost everywhere in Sudan you can find the line of *jelabiyahs* hung in the street that mark the dobyman's place of work. In the morning, he'll be pounding the clothes in a low tin basin by the door, his sleeves rolled up to reveal the leather amulets tied over the biceps; in the afternoon, you might catch him spitting water down on the sun-dried *jelabiyahs* so that the charcoal iron might leave a firmer crease.

When I stayed in the *laconda*, only two of the residents were from the South. I thought they might be in the army, for they had that kind of build, but it turned out they were graduates of Cairo University, working in health education. In contrast, many of the 'Arab' Sudanese in the hotel made a living hawking their wares from market to market – plastic cups and plastic jugs made in China, for there's hardly anything now in the *suqs* that is not made in China.

One day, one of the 'Arab' Sudanese called over one of the graduates and handed him his bundle of dirty clothes

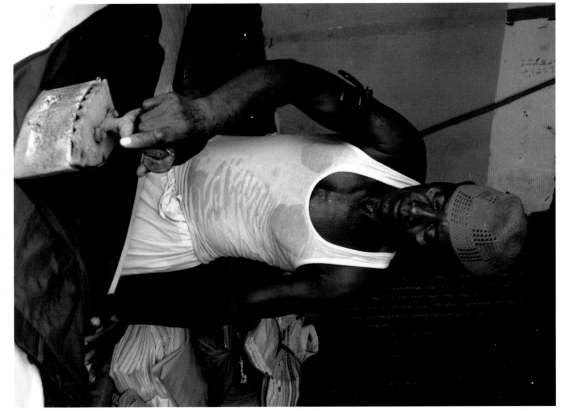

Dobyman in Damazine, Blue Nile State

to wash: a bit of a social blunder, perhaps, but such was the mind-set among those 'Arab' hawkers of plastic wares.

One of my 'Arab' Sudanese colleagues had a not dissimilar experience when attending a conference in my hometown in the north of Ireland. He was standing on the steps of the four-star hotel, having flown in business class from Sudan, wrapped up for the winter's day. A young woman stopped and greeted him.

'Tell me, are you working here in the kitchens?'

WITH THE DATE MERCHANTS OF OMDURMAN

As far as I could see it, it was the 'Arab' Sudanese traders who controlled much of Omdurman *Suq*. They only did the trading of course; it was the labourers from the west who unloaded the sacks of dates down from the lorries from Atbara and Karima and Dongola, their backs bent double as they hauled the produce to the stores. The *awlad al baher*, the 'people of the river', were the businessmen while the 'men of the west', the *awlad al ghareb*, did the labouring.

On winter mornings, the merchants sat and chatted in the doorways, huddled together on sacks, warming their hands with the sweet, milky tea that the Sudanese drink first thing in the morning, maybe tucking into a dish of sugared doughnuts at the same time. It could be several hours until breakfast; it is not unusual to have just two meals a day, a late breakfast around eleven and a late lunch around four.

In the afternoon, when I returned from my classes, the merchants would still be there, counting the day's takings. Outside in the heat of the day, half a dozen labourers, stripped to the waist, would be washing off the day's dust from a shared cooking oil tin in the street.

One day, the merchants called me into their store and asked me where I was from. When I said I was from Ireland one of the older merchants nodded knowingly and asked me to explain the fighting in Ireland. In reply, I asked him to tell me about the conflict in Sudan. They all laughed comfortably at my request, and one of the merchants expounded on the origins of the civil war in Sudan. A western view might be that relations between North and South existed for the pursuit of two 'commodities': slaves and ivory. The British intervened to stop the slave trade or, in today's parlance, to 'protect civilians'. In contrast, the usual version of history I would hear in Khartoum went something like this: we Sudanese were all living happily together until the British came along and divided our country.

This is not without factual basis. Under British rule it did become illegal for 'Arab' Sudanese to travel south of a certain parallel without documentation; there was

Labourers from Darfur in Omdurman Suq

a deliberate attempt to prevent the spread of Islam, and Christian missionaries were encouraged to set up schools in the South, where the only education available was a Christian one and English, not Arabic, was the official language. British policy was very much bent on creating a separate South Sudan. As independence neared, however, there was a reversal of policy; Sudan would be one. But as the civil service was Sudanized just before independence, of the 800 posts, only about half a dozen were given to Southern Sudanese. The Sudanese of the South were ditched and the next five decades were mostly dedicated to civil war.

Rather than considering the intricacies of British rule in the Sudan, where the South had been essentially handed over to the 'Bog Barons,' British administrators who ruled through the local chiefs – not an easy task given that some tribes were egalitarian and without chiefs – the merchant of the *suq* had a rather simple explanation concerning ethnicity and Sudan.

'It's like this,' he said. 'We're from the North and they're from the South. We're white, and they're black.'

I looked at the merchants in their immaculate cotton robes with amazement: these 'Arab' Northerners spoke of themselves as 'white', yet their complexion was only slightly lighter than say a Kenyan's. I said something I would not get away with in some other societies.

'The only thing "white" about your guys is your *jelabiyahs*!' And with their comfortable good-humoured nature they laughed at that as well.

In seeing themselves in some bizarre way as 'white', the date merchants were observing a Sudanese taboo: although 'Sudan' is said to mean 'Land of the Blacks', a name that must have originated externally, from, say, colonizing Arabs, not from within, there are few Sudanese from the North in my experience who would call themselves 'black', although a foreigner like me would see them as 'black' or African.

Colour is such a taboo topic it has bred a wealth of words: someone with a light complexion could be described as 'green'; one of my colleagues was called the Green Man. When people like me used a word like 'black', the Sudanese themselves would see 'blue' and so someone's complexion might be described as 'blue', as in, 'Give this to the blue-skinned one.' Did the Sudanese actually see a bluish tinge to the darkest complexions, just as I saw a hint of blue in the smoke rising from the brick kilns on the banks of the Nile, the Nuban brick-makers no doubt utterly at ease with an African identity?

This was the 'Arab'-Sudanese dilemma: they wanted to distance themselves from what was at the heart of the word 'Sudan': *sud*, the plural of *aswad* – 'black'.

Ironically, I sense sometimes that the feeling among the 'Arab' Sudanese, those dominant groups the Sudanese sometimes call *awlad al-baher* (the people of the Nile north of Khartoum like the Ja'aliyyin, the Shayqiyya and the Danaqala), is that they feel they are somehow the true Sudanese. Which takes us again to conflict and identity. When a group equates Sudanese identity with Arab-Muslim, they would not have seen the wars of Arabization and Islamization as against people they saw as essentially Sudanese.

How does this apply to Darfur? When I returned to Khartoum recently after some time in Nyala, one of those affable taxi drivers indolently reclining in his taxi asked me how it was in Darfur. When I spoke of the situation there, his response was to refer to the troublesome *abeed*, the slaves. To him, ethnic groups like the Fur were merely slaves, African slaves.

It's not very satisfactory talking about 'Arab' and 'African' Sudanese; who in Darfur, apart from the aid workers, are not African? Perhaps it would make more sense to look at ethnicity through language. There are those who speak Arabic as their first language and those whose first language is an indigenous African language — but even this is too simplistic, for there must be hundreds of thousands who in acquiring Arabic have lost to some extent their mother tongue, or maybe switch between

Brickmaker, Rosseires

to themselves as *zenuj* or blacks. They were, I believe, asking if we in Europe had the problem of the 'blacks' the way that they had with the Southerners.

I brought up the issue one day in Nyala, when I was invited by my trainees in the judiciary for breakfast. I had been rather dreading the occasion, fearing the stiff formality of armchairs and breakfast conversation. However, it all loosened up, with lots of banter and delicious local *assida* (like a heavy porridge) and fried chicken, and one of my hosts expressed his regret that my colleague Rasheed had not come too. The name rang a bell for one of the men present.

'I knew a man called Rasheed in Omdurman. Could this be the same Rasheed?' Something was then said enthusiastically about Rasheed and the Sufi brotherhood. I held back, and asked for clarification.

'I don't know. What does he look like?'

'He's big. And has a beard.'

'Yes, but what about his complexion?' Now there was considerable hesitation, for Rasheed, being a *khawaja* with Jamaican roots, presents something of a dilemma for the Sudanese. After careful consideration my trainee came out with his evaluation.

'Something between dark green and blue.'

I have once seen a man who could have been described as having green hints to his complexion, but that was in

Arabic at work and their mother tongue at home. In Sudan, indigenous languages are likely to be referred to as a mere *rutaana* or unwritten 'dialect', reflecting a pervasive ideology where languages other than Arabic are dismissed as something at best incomprehensible, if not utterly inferior.

Seeing some ethnic groups and languages as more indigenous than others is a dangerous game. 'Arab' Sudanese like the Ja'aliyyin might trace their roots back to Abbas, the uncle of the Prophet,[27] with Arabs moving south over centuries through Nubian lands further and further into Sudan, trading and intermarrying and displacing more indigenous groups as they settled. But what today could be more intrinsically Sudanese than the dialect of Arabic that is spoken here? Surely Sudanese Arabic must be seen as indigenous. It goes beyond language to the landscapes of Khartoum: what could be more Sudanese than the neem trees that shade the streets of the capital? But such trees were brought to Sudan by the likes of Kitchener to grace Khartoum's avenues. Khartoum's quintessential tree is Indian.

In Sudan it is usually others who are black. Right up in Gedaref near the Ethiopian border, some lads from the Gezira asked me over tea in the *suq*, 'Do you have *zenuj* in Ireland?' Although their skin was the colour of Nelson Mandela's, they were not referring

Ireland after a drinking friend of mine returned after a long weekend away with the rugby team.

There seemed to be one word that could not be said in polite circles in this 'Land of the Blacks', and I asked for confirmation.

'Is the word 'black' thought to be offensive in Sudan?' We waited for the judge to give his verdict. 'We can just say that God made them like that!'

Of course he used the pronoun 'them' not 'us', and no one in the room, Rasheed being absent, took offence, for no one saw themselves as 'black'. They were members of the judiciary and, therefore, from the 'Arab' Islamic traditions of the North. The Fur however, who were not represented among the judges that I met, would be seen as 'black'. Being 'black' in Sudan is not essentially about skin colour but ethnic group; the Fur would probably identify themselves as African, but the ruling groups, the *awlad al baher*, would tend to see themselves as 'Arab'.

The judge on my left, with the good looks that come from restrained living, dignified in the *imma* and *jelabiyah* appropriate for Friday prayers, laughed wholeheartedly.

'Now that would be a good name for a book: *God made them like that!*' I wondered for a moment, but within a couple of minutes everyone was standing up to leave. That is how it is in Sudan: you eat and leave.

The Sudanese denial of African-ness is almost a national occupation, in the North that is, but then I would see denial as a national characteristic, whether it is to deny the existence of malaria in Khartoum or the war in Darfur, which many like to present as something merely 'tribal'. You just have to pick up a newspaper to read the typical headline 'The Government denies...' In linguistic terms that's a strong collocation: if you have the noun 'government' you can expect the verb 'denies' to follow. Where the 'international community' place the number killed in Darfur as 300,000 or 400,000 depending on the source, with maybe 2,700,000 displaced, the Khartoum government has put the death toll at 10,000.[28]

I would have to admit, however, that when it came to culture, trainees in Khartoum would feel much more at home with cultural references relating to Cairo or the Middle East than to Nairobi or Kampala. Arabic as the mother tongue would be the primary factor here, but I'm sure in school curricula there has been a conscious effort to reinforce, if not create in some areas, an 'Arab' identity.

The matter with the date merchants, however, didn't end there with their black and white explanation of Sudanese history. Another day in the *suq* one of the merchants leaned out of his pick-up and called me over.

'Would you like to meet one of the pure Arabs of Sudan?'

'I'd be delighted!'

'Well, you don't have far to look. He's sitting here right next to me!'

The young man in the passenger seat did not much resemble any member of the House of Saud. In fact, he looked to me more like the Fur labourers of Darfur working in the *suq*.

'Would you not say that your friend's complexion is perhaps a little dark for an Arab?'

'Skin colour is not the issue!'

'And the nose? Would you not say that your friend's nose is perhaps more typical of an African's than an Arab's?'

We were clearly getting onto dangerous ground here, but the guy laughed with good humour, for political correctness has yet to suffocate conversation in Sudan.

'Haven't you noticed his hair?' I had to concede that his companion's hair was not typically Afro, but then, in my mind, neither was it the flowing locks of the bedouin.

My lesson on ethnicity in Sudan was now coming to an end. Was he mocking his friend, or was it the priggish foreigner who was being mocked? Or was he actually, in his urbane way, laughing at Sudanese pretensions to being 'Arab'?

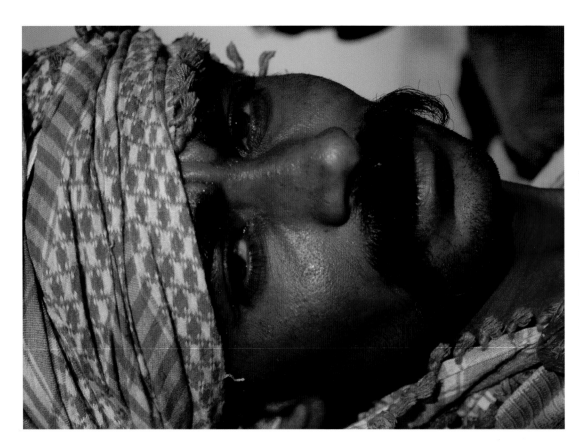

Portrait in a village outside Khartoum

One of my trainees in Blue Nile State recounted how, on arriving in Syria, he had joined the queue at immigration that was for Arabs only, only to find himself initially directed elsewhere by a Syrian official. But the police officer told his story with laughter, comfortable with the re-adjustment of identity that was needed on leaving Sudan.

My personal guide to ethnicity in Sudan was hardly suffering from angst as he gave his final mocking words on the issue of ethnicity.

'So now, *ya khawaja*, you know how to identify a pure Arab in Sudan: it's the hair!'

THE ATTRACTIONS OF SUDAN

I could say it was Islam that attracted me, the way it shaped daily life: those minarets by the Nile, the dawn call to prayer sounding out when I slept outside in the yard, the men lining up for prayers, the rhythms of Islam shaping the day. But that would not be entirely honest.

I could see the appeal of Islam: the discipline it would give, going to the mosque in the half-light for dawn prayers; the sense of belonging as you joined your neighbours in a row on the pavement for communal prayer later in the day; the completion of the day with a bowing down before the Creator.

It was not just the day, for the year, too, would be shaped by Ramadan and the festivals. And life itself: the *bismillah* on the birth of a baby, through to the *hamdillallah* as life ended with burial in a simple shroud. It must be comforting to live with all the questions of life answered in the 'complete knowledge' believed to have been revealed to the Prophet.

But then there were those unanswered questions related to what was being done in the name of Islam in Sudan. Such events could not be taking place without the ideologies to support them, ideologies that I hoped were a deviation from Islam, and contrary to Islam, rather than an expression of Islamic teachings, just as actions committed in the Crusades would have been utterly against the teachings of the gospels. And then there was my own upbringing: although I had absorbed, I hope, some of the values of the Muslim Sudanese, why would I, being from the north of Ireland, want to exchange one system of fundamentalist belief for another?

Almost all of my Sudanese friends were Muslim. In Khartoum, I hardly knew anyone from the South, although the dispossessed had fled north in their millions. I never had the same rapport with the Southerners, or at least the dispossessed as I encountered them in Khartoum, even though I knew that they were very much wronged. Was it their looks, or their Arabic, or the desperate circumstances of their lives? I felt much more affinity with the Muslim-'Arab' Sudanese.

I never much empathized with the Christians of Khartoum. Apart from some of the Nubans I hardly knew them, although I'd see them gathering by their churches. They had permission to do that, but were forbidden to put up a new church building. The Copts seemed a rather insular lot, and as for the Sudanese of the South, I would have been more interested in their indigenous beliefs than what had been imported from Europe or the USA.

With their immediate hospitality, and their affable natures, not to mention their stunning looks – the loose folds of their *jelabiyahs* setting off the dark grain of the skin, the sleeve maybe folded up to half-reveal the leather charm above the biceps if they were from the west – it would be more honest to say it was the Muslims of Sudan who attracted me.

AN ENCOUNTER ON THE ROAD

Travelling down from Wadi Halfa near the border with Egypt back to Khartoum, I passed through a landscape of desert rock and sand with an occasional green glimpse of the Nile and its lush islands.

These were the Nubian lands, lands that had paid tribute to the Pharaohs, then become Christian and then submitted to Islam. Somehow they have retained their culture although some of the richest agricultural land – the narrow strip between the Nile and desert rock – is flooded by the dam built for hydro-electric power and the border divides them from the Nubians of Egypt. Being speakers of a so-called *rutaana* rather than Arabic, they are also marginalized from the centres of power in Khartoum.

It was that time of year when, between the rock and Nile waters, lush fields of corn were ripening. The men were harvesting, an uneven line across the field, stooping down to grasp the corn in one hand and scythe it with a hook held in the other. Further down the road, they were winnowing the harvested crops, the chaff clouding the air beneath the palms. Sometimes, I'd stop and interrupt them in their work and they'd offer me a drink of water as we chatted indolently at the field's edge.

I had planned to travel to Ed Debba and then get the steamer for a day or so along the Nile to Karima. But as we crossed the desert, the driver was in no hurry. We'd stop in the shade of some *rokuba* and he'd lie back on the woven *angarib* bed and sip tea while we waited for him to feel refreshed. I had hoped to travel in some old steamer that had seen better days, calling with the post from village to village among the encroaching dunes, but instead I travelled overland in pickups and buses. I missed the boat. I never had the chance again; you can find the steamers now beached on a bank of the Nile at Karima, discarded like the trains with which they once connected.

As we journeyed, there was that kind of closeness that is normal on the road. Crushed together in the back of the pickup, bathing in the Nile to wash off the accumulated dust, sleeping outside the mosque one night when there was no *laconda* in which to stay, how could some companionship not have developed among travellers?

Reaching a town, we carried the beds out into the yard of the hotel, sleeping a few feet apart under the fluorescent lights of the courtyard, for it was too hot to sleep inside. Sometimes when you are travelling you meet up with someone on the way, and it is this, more than anything else, that makes travel worthwhile.

In the morning, as it was time to go our separate ways, after we had exchanged addresses and were shaking hands in parting – it is strange that I should have forgotten his name – my fellow-traveller left an unexpected kiss on the neck. It was just a farewell among casual companions who had travelled a bit on the road

Ferryman, Kerma Mahas, Nubia

together, eaten from the same dish and maybe drunk from the same tin can by the *zeer* when we stopped, but I was left not so much with a farewell as with a sense of loss, of life unfulfilled. It was like when you are living in the city and catch sight of a full moon low in the sky, there above the street with its pizza places and burger joints – not that warm amber moon you see sometimes in an autumnal sky at home, but a pure, cold circle in the sky, a desert moon, haunting you with thoughts of the life you have not had the courage to live: something more poignant than a mere photograph not taken.

NOTES

1   Wyndham, Richard, *The Gentle Savage: A Sudanese Journey in the Province of Bahr-el-Ghazal, commonly called 'The Bog'* (New York: Negro Universities Press, 1970) p.29

2   Ibid. p.36

3   Power, Frank, *Letters from Khartoum Written During the Siege* (London: Sampson Low, Marston, Searle & Rivington, 1885) p.18

4   Fothergill, Edward, *Five Years in the Sudan* (London: Hurst & Blackett, 1910) p.43

5   Baker, Samuel, *In the Heart of Africa*. Project Gutenberg, www.gutenberg.org/3233

6   Thesiger, Wilfred, *Arabian Sands* (London: Harper Collins, 2000) p.15.

7   Ibid.

8   Power, op. cit. p.24

9   Thompson, Brian, *Imperial Vanities* (Harper Collins, 2002) p.202

10 Ibid. p.202

11 Burckhardt, John Lewis, *Travels in Nubia* (London: John Murray, 1819) p.341

12 Ibid. p.360

13 Churchill, Winston, *The River War: An Account of the Reconquest of the Sudan* (London: Longmans, Green and Co. 1902). Project Gutenberg, www.gutenberg.org/3233

14 Thompson, op. cit. p.250

15 Collins, op. cit. p.197

16 Slatin, Rudolph, *Fire and Sword in the Sudan* (Geneva: The Long Riders' Guild Press, 2006) p.334

17 Churchill, op. cit.

18 Kapuscinski, Ryszard, *The Shadow of the Sun* (Penguin, 2002) p.196

19 Collins, op. cit. p.170

20 Churchill, op. cit.

21 Kapuscinski, op. cit. p.195

22 Crilly, Robert, *Saving Darfur: Everyone's Favourite War* (Reportage Press, 2010)

23 Salih, Tayeb, *Season of Migration to the North* (Heinemann, 1991) p.3

24 Baker, op. cit.

25 Collins, op. cit. p.147

26 Kapuscinski, Ryszard, *Travels with Herodotus* (Penguin, 2007) p.120

27 Fadl, Yusuf, *The Arabs and The Sudan From the Seventh to the Early Sixteenth Century* (SUDATeK Ltd., 2010) p.146

28 BBC News: Q&A: 'Sudan's Darfur conflict', 23rd February 2010, www.bbc.co.uk/2/hi/africa/3496731.stm

CHAPTER TWO

INTO THE MYSTIC

I never quite knew what to make of the Sufis who gather on Fridays at the tomb of Sheikh Hamid el Nil in Omdurman. Hamid el Nil was a mystic whose body was recovered from the waters of the Nile in a state of perfection. Many days after his death the sheikh's body had not decomposed; today the Sudanese still gather at his tomb on a Friday afternoon to commemorate the holy man.

The sheikh's tomb rises exotically like the mausoleum of some Maharaja transferred to the outskirts of a Sudanese town, surrounded by the little mounds of other graves with their piece of tin to mark the spot, the deceased all directed towards Mecca, so that believers might rise together on the Day of Judgement. As people gather to watch the Sufis perform (and it is in some sense a performance) girls sit by the headstones to sell groundnuts, as if a graveyard were the most natural place in the world to set up shop.

Within the half-light of the mausoleum, devotees raise their hands in prayer for his soul, women on the left, men on the right, and maybe take some dust from his burial place in the hope of his blessing or *baraka*. This is Islam at its most Catholic; they hope the righteous soul will intercede for them with God.

Outside the tomb that Friday quite a crowd were hanging around waiting for something to happen; in Sudan, a lot of the day is spent just waiting. A few dubious types were entertaining the idle by circling with a tambourine and chanting; the support group before the main Sufi act.

Eventually, the sheikhs and their entourage arrived in a swirl of green banners, golden script declaring their faith, drummers quickening the pace of things. Under the tomb, it was all greetings and joyful embraces, as if the sheikhs hadn't seen each other for years, although they had probably met just the previous Friday. The

Tomb of Hamid el Nil

crescendo of drumming ended in a sudden raising of hands in supplication.

There was a circle, mostly of barefooted men clad in white *jelabiyahs*, their shoes cast within the ring, for this was holy ground. Moving backwards and forwards slightly, they slowly chanted the declaration of faith as the sheikhs gathered within. One did the rounds, ordering this one in the ranks further back, shouting at another, imposing order with an occasional tap with a stick or even the flip of a whip.

Things were slow in warming up. '*La allah il Allah*' was being chanted, but without any vigour, and the master of ceremonies was urging the lads to put a bit of life into it. Some days the Sufis just never quite get going.

I have seen the Dervishes in Damascus where they perform in immaculate white, their skirts rising to create a world within which the 'worshipper' rotates. But it is sanitized and secularized, even performed in a restaurant to entertain the diners: ritual without soul. In Sudan, the Sufis certainly have soul.

At Hamid el Nil they were a motley crew. One sheikh in a *jelabiyah* had entered the circle alone and was blissfully gliding along, benign in his smiles. Another looked anxiously towards the tomb, frown marks permanently etched on his forehead. And then there were the epileptics and the 'simple' wandering

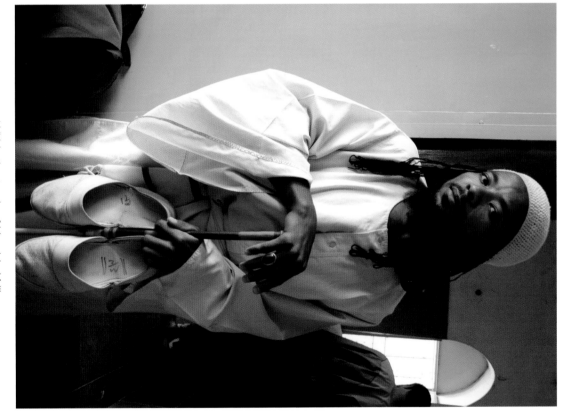

Within the tomb of Hamid el Nil

within the circle; the Sufis see such people as especially gifted and on another plane.

It all seemed rather incongruous to me. When I thought of the dark-suited sobriety of the Presbyterian elders of my upbringing, with the minister in his black robes, what was I to make of the middle-aged sheikh kitted out in a pink raffia skirt for his act of worship? Where was the dignity of religion?

I gazed sceptically at the spectacle before me. Was I to believe that the apparent simpleton wandering within the Sufi ring, welcomed within the sacred circle, would somehow lead us all to God? I had forgotten that text learnt in my youth about praise coming 'out of the mouth of babes and sucklings', but Tayeb Salih perhaps reflects a particularly Sudanese view in writing that our hope of salvation is to be found 'in the rough wisdom that issues from the mouths of simple people'.[1] One dreadlocked devotee was brought into the circle in his wheelchair.

There was something attractively inclusive about the Sufis. At Hamid el Nil, non-Muslims were welcome – this was Khartoum's main tourist attraction, with maybe a dozen foreigners present – and although nowadays only men paraded within the circle, women clearly had their half of the tomb. In Sufi traditions there have been respected female sheikhs instructing the women of their community.

The Sufis were difficult to categorize. Most seemed to speak a very working-class Arabic, but some could have been merchants in the *suq*. Sufi traditions are an integral part of life across the Sudan, from the far west where traditions were brought by the Nigerian founder of a Sufi order, to the east, with the founder of the Khatmiyya order originating from the Hejaz.

Sufism may have been brought to Sudan some five centuries ago, but nothing seems more indigenous to Sudan than the Sufi approach to religion. I have seen a dervish wandering alone with just his beads and water jar for ablutions in Kordofan; I have also met a dreadlocked Sufi who was a landlord renting out his spacious villa in Omdurman. Sufism permeates Sudanese life. That day I came across one Sufi sitting among the graves fondling a cat and he explained that his day job was that of *ustaz* or teacher. This, of course, was an appropriate vocation for a Sufi, but he then went on to explain that he was a martial arts coach.

Below the branches of an acacia tree, the devotees of one sheikh were kitted out in green and red, like a visiting football team. Very African in their features, some sported dreadlocks that would be the envy of the coolest Londoner. They were now getting into the way of things, moving in a way that was almost synchronised. I was witnessing a *dhikar*, a ritual of Sufi worship, an act of remembering God. The movements had begun with a gentle swaying of the body from right to left and progressed to a slow flexing of the legs so that the body was lowered, the worshippers communally repeating the word 'Allah'. Now things had quickened to what seemed to be an energetic thrusting of the body as the devotees called upon God. To an outsider, the movements suggested that a certain physical energy was being sublimated. To the Sufi believer, however, the movement expressed his worshipping God not just with his mind but with his entire self, body and soul, hoping to reach some ecstatic point of communion with the Divine.

Sufi mystics have often expressed their relationship with God in the language of love, but we do not have to go to Khartoum for this concept: within the sedate Church of England, deans and vicars such as the poets John Donne and George Herbert have used outrageous imagery to describe their relationship with God. Here, at dusty Hamid el Nil, the rhythm peaked and the lines of men were still.

On one occasion I have seen a devotee collapse in the dust where he lay dead to the world, enjoying a state of ecstasy. I suppose he had reached some other state of consciousness, for the Sufis are believed to attain a personal union with God, a belief that is anathema to

Sufi worshipper at Hamid el Nil

Sufis participating in a *dhikar*

Sufis participating in a *dhikar*

They carried him off somewhere to come down to earth.

This was clearly a very Africanized Islam. The act of worship was a world apart from the legalistic observances of some Islamic groups which seemed to me to emphasize outward behaviour at the expense of the spiritual, as if outward observance and the fastidious adherence to details of a legal code were everything. Sufism in Sudan can be seen as a popular, even rural, rejection of the legalistic Islam that has been imported from Egypt and Saudi Arabia. If the mosque in Sudan tends to orientate believers towards a legalistic observance of a code, then the domed tomb, rising from the landscape and sometimes composed of indigenous building materials from that landscape, reflects a popular Islam that is a grassroots expression of the spiritual.

It was hard to reconcile the benevolent Islam that I saw in the Sufis at Hamid el Nil with the Dervishes of over a century ago, when General Gordon became a British martyr at the hands, or spears, of the Mahdi's warriors. In contrast to those days, nothing could be more genial than this afternoon's gathering, with foreigners warmly tolerated, even embraced. There was something, however, that jarred: in the context of contemporary Sudan, why was the sheikh in the fake leopard skin carrying a replica gun?

Reaching a state of ecstasy

some. Sufis follow a *tariqah*, or spiritual way, expressed in the teachings of their sheikh. Compared to his journey my travels were nothing, and I stared at his outstretched body with disbelief. A passing Sufi was somewhat less impressed. '*Mapsout!*' he called out, with that lovely Sudanese irreverence. The equivalent I suppose would be for some minister of an evangelical church to call out as a fellow worshipper was taken by the spirit, 'Getting high are we?'

Sufi banner

At the *mulid*

Inhaling the incense, Hamid el Nil

Soon the chanting started again, but this time all was tranquil. One Sufi wearing the jester patches of the dervish was holding an incense burner of charcoal for spectators to breathe in a cloud of incense, and I suspect that among some present it is not just incense that is sometimes inhaled.

A devotee knelt at the feet of one sheikh, holding an incense burner beneath his skirts to scent his clothes. Again, something within me jarred. Where in this Sufi congregation was the levelling democracy of Islam? From my own Presbyterian traditions the leader of the community would be someone elected by a committee, selected for the job as it were, with none of the authority granted to say a priest. Similarly, Islam is, in theory, the most democratic of religions, although a Sudanese working in Saudi Arabia might find himself far down a well-established pecking order. In Islam no priest acts as an intermediary between God and mankind and even someone with the most menial of jobs can lead the community in prayer. Why was a Sufi now kneeling before a religious leader, scenting his clothes, as if he were a prince?

At the *mulid*, the celebration of the Prophet's birthday, in the square near the Mahdi's tomb in Omdurman, I have seen this personality cult of the sheikhs, and it has grated with what I have absorbed from Islam in

Sufis of the Samaniya brotherhood arriving
at the square before the Mahdi's Tomb

other cultures. The festival has the atmosphere of a fair, with candyfloss and popcorn and fairy lights. In the square, different sheikhs have their own dedicated areas, marking off their area with canvas. To me it is not unlike Freshers' Week at a university in the UK, with different groups competing for the recruitment of the new arrivals, each amplifying its presence through loudspeakers so that there's a cacophony of sound. In this case, however, it's not the fresh undergraduate but the uneducated lad from the Gezira, dazzled by the

Sufis of the Samaniya brotherhood worshipping at the *mulid*, Omdurman

dancing synthetic flames that sometimes brighten shop windows but are used here to hint of the miraculous, who is the targeted recruit.

Pink candies in the shape of brides and riders on horses are the souvenirs of the *mulid* and thousands of people mill around in the square. There is even a hint of the Hari Krishna as joyous worshippers hit cymbals above their heads. But above it all, towering above the dusty crowds, are the portraits of certain sheikhs who claim to lead others in their spiritual way. Again, it's a very Sudanese form of Islam, this veneration of the sheikh, something that goes back beyond the time of the Mahdi, who had himself been the disciple of a Sufi sheikh.

To me, aspects of the *mulid*, such as the giant-sized portraits of sheikhs, seemed more appropriate to electioneering than Islam, for in Islam the portrayal of the human form in the context of worship is something absolutely *haram* or forbidden. And the resemblance to a political campaign is hardly coincidental; adherence to a certain *tariqah* or way might also imply following a certain political path.

The *mulid* is the great gathering together of different Sufi brotherhoods. A couple of days before the *mulid* officially began, I had seen the Samaniya Sufis arrive in festive mood, their leaders on horseback, their followers exuberantly passing through the gates beneath a swirl of banners, to line up where mats are spread out for the *dhikar*. In contrast to the ragtag get-together at Hamid el Nil, the Samaniya Sufis worship in spotless *jelabiyahs* and skullcaps, absolutely immaculate.

The venue for the *mulid* could not be more appropriate: the silver-domed tomb of the Mahdi rises above the dusty square and the home of the Khalifa touches it. The worshippers stand in facing parallel lines and such is their respectability I think not of the Mahdi's followers, the *Ansar*, but of civil servants and accountants, the middle-aged among them perhaps reliving something of their youth, ceremoniously wearing leather belts across the stomach over their white robes.

The gradual flexing of the knees builds up until (like those Maasai of the African plains) they jump into the air, the chanting sounding out over the loudspeakers now a rasping expiration of air. Being respectable citizens of Omdurman, the Samaniya Sufis leap in a controlled, almost choreographed way, for even in their leaping they are dignified. In the exuberance of their worshipping I think of those words of another mystic, Yeats.

Seventy years have I lived,
Seventy years man and boy,
And never have I danced for joy.[2]

In contrast to the decorum of the Samaniya brotherhood, what was I to make of it all here at Hamid el Nil? Was the whole event mere exhibitionism, the entertaining of a crowd? Did some perhaps see it as an opportunity to con the simple, the naïf parting with their hard-earned cash in the belief that some sheikh possessed *baraka*, and the proffered amulet, like a talisman, would protect the wearer from ill-harm?

Observing the *dhikar*, I was witnessing an expression of Islam that would be anathema to some Muslims; the *mulid* has even been physically attacked by extremists who set up their own rival area within the tented enclosure, to declaim the celebrations around them. Just as Christmas celebrations were banned in Oliver Cromwell's England in the mid-seventeenth century as Puritans tried to 'purify' Christianity, so Salafis oppose the *mulid* as a celebration of the Prophet's birthday, seeing it as an unislamic *bid'ah* or innovation that was not practised by the first generation of Muslims.

The *amjad* driver who would take me from the event expressed his disapproval of the Sufis, for some see them as having deviated from 'true Islam'. I could see their point: the worshipping at a tomb; the 'miracles' performed by a sheikh; the belief that a dead sheikh could intercede with God so that a woman would be blessed with children when her husband had failed to

Sufi at Hamid el Nil

Worshipping at the *mulid*, Khartoum

provide any. With my Presbyterian upbringing, I could see the Salafi point of view on this one, but observing the dour opponents of Sufism who had set up their Trojan horse within the *mulid* itself, the Sufi way of life seemed even more attractive.

Now the Sufis were about to submit to one of the orthodox rituals of their religion. The sun was low in the sky, a dusty disc, and the lads viewing it all from the walls of the tomb were now in dark profile. It would all culminate with the call to prayer when everything would suddenly come to a halt and worshippers would gather by the taps to do their unhurried ablutions.

Until that moment, though, the circle of men would shout their declaration of faith, heads thrown back in communal ecstasy. One sheikh was leaping around the circle, doing his own thing. Another spun on his own axis, apparently oblivious to the material world, the centre of his own sacred circle. The leopard-skinned sheikh whirled expertly, dreadlocks framing his spinning head.

It was hard to reconcile this Islamic tolerance with the far from dulcet tones sounding out from some mosques at Friday prayers. This version of Islam was far removed from the forms of Islam that seem to have been imported from Egypt or from Saudi Arabia, severe in their austerity, extreme in their politics and marked by intolerance of other forms of religious expression.

In a country where so much seemed given over to the public observance of things religious (you could scarcely say a sentence in Arabic without some pious reference) I would sometimes ask myself what spirituality existed behind the public conformity. To me, it was the Sufis who conveyed something that reflected an individual's faith, expressing something spiritual rather than just conforming to public ritual.

Nothing could be more removed from my own religious upbringing than the Sufis: the doing your own thing; the exuberance; the worship through the gyrations of the body as well as through the normal rituals of prayer; the attainment by some of a state of ecstasy; the inclusiveness. At Hamid el Nil, despite the disapproval that the more officious might express, I was witnessing grassroots Islam in Sudan.

NOTES

1 Salih, op. cit. p.41

2 Yeats, William Butler, 'Imitated From the Japanese', *The Collected Poems of W.B. Yeats* (London: Macmillan, 1977) p. 340

CHAPTER THREE

THE MEN OF THE NINETY-NINE MOUNTAINS

Images of the Nuban wrestlers of Kordofan are for me the iconic photographs of Africa. Having celebrated in film the beauty of the athletes of Hitler's Olympic Games, Leni Riefenstahl found herself ostracized. Retreating to Kordofan, she documented in still photographs those other men of power and beauty: the Warriors of Kau.

Another photographer, George Rodger, had preceded Riefenstahl. After documenting the concentration camps of Europe, he travelled to Africa to search for another way of living, seeking, 'some spot in the world that was clean and untrammelled'.[1] He found it, he believed, 'in the fabulous land of the Nubas', where villages were so integrated with the natural landscape it seemed they had been thrown against the mountain rock. For Rodger, the Nuba Mountains were a strange, unreal land hardly touched by the passing of time.[2] Humanity seemed to be in some natural state, as he observed the Nubans gather for their wrestling contests.

I have also witnessed the Nuban wrestling contests in Kordofan. There in the Land of the Ninety-nine Mountains, the village homes are still mud huts growing out of the rock. The wrestlers wear a bunch of twigs like a tail, and the women cheer on their favourites from beneath the trees. It was strange for me to sit under a tree where a bow and arrows had been left, set there by a wandering Falata herder, and know that missiles and Kalashnikovs were the weapons of the war not many miles away.

Rodger went to Kordofan in search of an innocent humanity and felt that he had found it in the Nuban life he documented, even though the Nubans in some contests wore brass bracelets with which they would gash the flesh of their opponents.

Recent history in Kordofan has been anything but humane. The Nubans fought on both sides in the civil war, some with the Sudan People's Liberation Army

(SPLA) and some with Khartoum's Sudan Armed Forces (SAF). The conflict tore South Kordofan apart. A Nuban colleague of mine told me how the school where he was teaching was bombed from the air, but it is difficult to identify a school from a plane.

Although I had travelled in Kordofan, I really knew the Nubans not from their picturesque villages but from the shanty towns of Khartoum, where they lived in houses built of sun-dried mud, straw and dung in Umbedda and Angola in the outskirts of Omdurman. There, the donkeys deliver water in barrels, and an oil lamp or a wick stuck into a can would light their homes in the evenings. In those days, in the late-1980s, they held their contests at Hamid el Nil just a few minutes' walk away from the Dervishes. It seemed to me then that in some way the Sufis embodied some quest of the soul, but the Nubans celebrated the body.

That was a different generation of wrestlers: there was Bulubulu, named after an outrageous female singer who married an officer; then there was Silik – the Knife – and Civil Defence, named after the military force that was part of the 'jihad' of those days. But I hear they are all dead now: Bulubulu, who was the strongest and loveliest of them all, died from his injuries after being thrown in Port Sudan; Silik, who threw him, I heard, died of some

unidentified illness. Theirs were brief lives but not without moments of glory.

Nowadays, the Nuban wrestling takes place not near Hamid el Nil but in *Suq Sitta* beyond the banks of the Nile where so many Nubans work baking the mud bricks in kilns. The setting records the changes of a generation; they are urban dwellers now, but may return seasonally to the villages to graze the cattle.

The landscapes in Rodger's black-and-white photographs show wrestlers beneath baobabs; Riefenstahl's warriors are framed by the key-hole shaped doorway to a hut or pose theatrically on rocky summits. The landscape I know is a tented enclosure with the riot police eyeing the contest from their vehicles, the minaret of a newish mosque and a steel structure that looks like a communications tower rising above the canvas that rings the wrestling arena.

I sometimes wonder if there are more Nubans now in Khartoum than in Kordofan; it seems at times as if all Sudan has come to the capital, leaving the provinces to the old to manage. It's not just the regions wasted by war that villagers abandon for the city; those looking for work drift to the capital. Some will be absorbed into the army, some join the police and some will burn bricks.

Rodger delighted in the contests of Kordofan and the Nubans were appropriately decked out for the occasion. The wrestlers wore just a covering of wood ash, and maybe a small brass bell dangling from a leather thong around the waist. The female spectators merely covered their bodies in sesame oil. Rarely, even in Sudan, has the exotic been so erotic.

Today in Khartoum, the wrestlers are likely to appear in football shirts, branded not with the tattoos formed from cuts rubbed with wood ash to form raised zigzags and welts of the skin, but with the name of a mobile phone company or the like. There doesn't seem to be much of a dress code and, as if compensating for earlier laxities, where an earlier generation would have worn nothing, or at most a bunch of twigs covering the buttocks, now a wrestler might wear two pairs of shorts, the shorter over the longer. For the Nubans the body has been something to be displayed, not hidden in shame.

Nowadays, a wrestler might sport a dangling pompon or two from the waist, given by his lover. Also, leather amulets are often tied tight across the biceps, containing a sacred verse to protect from harm, or from the Eye. These amulets are not unique to wrestling but are common in Kordofan, worn to protect from a knife, or in war a bullet, or even a scorpion's sting.

When Rodger witnessed the wrestling contests, there were maybe half a dozen pairs of wrestlers fighting at once, and it was hard, in the general mêlée, to distinguish between wrestlers and spectators. The Nuban tradition, in which champions fought for the honour of their village, has now become a commercialized sport: there are referees, a ticket costs two Sudanese pounds (twice the price of a glass of tea) and the upwardly mobile can hire a chair for an additional pound.

The wrestling ring is not a roped-off platform as in the west, but a wide circle drawn in the dust. Just as the Sufis have their sacred circle in pursuit of the divine, so the Nubans have their circle in which the body itself is celebrated. I've never quite worked out the rules: for some reason there are two officials refereeing the contests, one primarily acting as time-keeper, often dressed in luminescent lime. They suffer a barrage of insults if a decision is made that contradicts the crowd's sense of fair play or their bias. I only know that the wrestlers can't go outside the outermost circle and the goal is not so much to hold the opponent in a painful grasp as in western wrestling but to somehow lift him. If both feet are off the ground the opponent is likely to be thrown to an ignominious end in the dust and the contest is won.

After the afternoon call to prayer, teams arrive at opposite ends of the field. I'm a supporter of the 'Lion Hearts' club, whose champion is Kerubino. He has

Nuban wrestlers at *Suq Sitta*

taken the name of a notorious warlord, but then the wrestlers are not without a black humour in the names they adopt: Bird Flu, the Fan (such do his arms rotate), Kosti Bridge (such is the width of the man, he could stretch across the Nile).

Like everything else in Sudan, this event takes a while to get started. Eventually, a couple of members of one team line up and dare their opponents sitting in a bunch across the way. They do not so much challenge as taunt, rising from their hunkers to spread their arms and show the palms of their hands to their opponents, imitating animal calls as they do so. Someone from the opposing team will eventually choose one and challenge him. If the challenge is accepted, there is a quick scattering of dust over the body and the contest begins.

Kerubino has patience. He taunts dexterously, moving in a way that denies his rival any kind of grip. It might be ages before a throw – the method is often to try and goad the rival into action with, for example, an adept slap to the head that provokes the opponent to anger and leaves him vulnerable. Nuban wrestling is not so much about strength as about craft. The slow giant Degaga, who occasionally visits the capital from Kordofan, replete with a diet of fresh milk, is an unusual champion; it is normally the slight but crafty winner who delights the crowd.

Kerubino, champion wrestler

Traditional pose

There is none of the acting of US wrestling on TV, and sportsmanship rules; here, even as he gets up painfully from the dust, the fallen affably shakes the hand of the victor. The winner is then likely to be hoisted on the shoulders of another wrestler, perhaps even the opponent he has thrown, and carried triumphantly around the arena to the applause of the crowd.

In one of Rodger's photographs from the late-1940s, the victor, wearing nothing but a bracelet and a single ear-ring, is carried on the shoulders of another wrestler, who good-humouredly parades the champion, the victor and the vanquished forever paired together, their physiques perfect. Today, Kerubino would make a fine model for a contemporary Michelangelo's Adam.

If anything, Nuban wrestling is a celebration of maleness, and there is a certain homoeroticism to Rodger's image; there is both strength and intimacy in its naked pairing of two men. But how should the photograph be read? In contemporary linguistics there is the issue of whether the meaning of a passage is extracted from the text, or whether readers create meaning through the life experiences they bring to the text. Perhaps photography is no different. I suspect the Nubans themselves would have found Rodger's image about as erotic as the sight of two European businessmen clinching a deal with a handshake.

The winning contestants may enjoy financial rewards from the crowd; a handful of notes, usually of the lower denominations, are often slapped on the forehead one by one. The wrestlers also get a share of the money collected at the gate, but I doubt that they are the major beneficiaries. I suspect the victor of an important contest would traditionally have been rewarded by pairing up at an appropriate time with the choicest of the females at the gathering. There does, however, seem to be a link between celibacy and wrestling; around the time of contests, in order to preserve their 'power', the men abstain from intercourse, or so I have been told.

Rodger writes of the apparently casual nature of relationships among the Nubans of his day; it was a way of life that seemed free and uninhibited.[3] A couple were bound together not with a marriage certificate but with the spoken word and their mutual agreement. Other Sudanese tribes, such as the Dinka, mark marriage by the transfer of cattle from the bride's family to the groom's, and with the receipt of the cows the marriage

The victor is carried on another's shoulders

Sudani embraces his opponent

is sealed. The Nubans, however, are cultivators more than pastoralists, and I have never heard of cows being a required dowry. I'm sure Rodger's words still hold true today.

Such indigenous traditions have been incompatible with Sudan's status as an 'Islamic' state. In just one or two generations, the majority of the Nubans have been to some extent Islamized, although that does not mean that everyone has given up their liking for the local *marissah* beer or ardently fasts in Ramadan. But one evening over supper in my flat, Kerubino surprised me: when I mentioned Ramadan he said he was a Christian.

Theirs is a culture at odds with the Arab-Islamic systems of the North and also, perhaps, with the Dinka-dominated culture of the South. But who can say they are more Sudanese than the Nubans? Once in Khartoum, maybe it was because of the smart casual clothes that he wears, or because of his build, someone in 'Security' stopped Kerubino and demanded proof of Sudanese nationality. The man was lucky not to have been thrown to the pavement, but Kerubino's build is matched by his mildness of manner. Despite the implication that Sudan was not his country, he maintained his good humour and produced his own version of an ID. He simply pulled down his lower lip and exposed the absence of certain incisors. Rather than have an initiation rite such as circumcision, the Nubans have tended, traditionally, not to remove the foreskin but certain teeth.

I have never seen Kerubino defeated, but I have seen him close to fainting after a difficult contest. No one can match his strength and agility in the ring, and he will often be hoisted on a contestant's shoulders to be paraded before the spectators. Often, a few wrestlers will do a victory circle of the field, one clutching a Sudanese flag with SUDAN in English (Arabization still has some distance to go) written across it. The Nubans are being embraced by the state, and over the loudspeakers the event is described not as Nuban wrestling but as 'Sudanese wrestling', a strange term to me, for I had thought of the tradition as belonging to the Nubans alone.

The Nuban contests now are less violent than before; they no longer entail the deep cuts from the chunky bracelets that Rodger witnessed in some Nuban fighting contests. They are also more exclusively male. Before, there used to be quite a few women among the spectators, but with the 'embrace' of Islam, there is hardly a woman in the crowd, except for the girls moving before the rows of spectators with the bags of seeds that people split between their teeth, spitting out the husks on to the ground.

Some days, such as when there is a visiting dignitary from Turkey, where they have their own wrestling and where at least one Ottoman sultan had been a champion wrestler, the cheerleaders, some looking more like aunties than girlfriends, parade around the field and chant from the sidelines to the sound of drums and men blowing through horns in support.

Rodger, succumbing to the warmth and good humour of the Nubans, found them to be naturally decent people. There seemed to be little conventional religion among them, and he commented that, given their good natures and their honesty, perhaps they didn't need orthodox religion to make them better people.[4] However, as we know, there is always room for improvement and the Nubans have been 'embraced' by Islam and, to a lesser extent, Christianity.

Once, when the cheerleaders were sounding it out, a bearded spectator in Arab dress turned to me.

'*Ya, khawaja…*' The way he intoned the word for 'foreigner' hinted at what was to follow.

'Do you know what they are saying?' I understood what he was getting at.

'Indeed I do. They're not chanting in Chinese are they?'

He had good reason to be smug. In supporting the wrestlers, the female supporters of the Lion Hearts

team were calling out their declaration of faith. Even the wrestling has been Islamized and a Nuban contest is seen as an appropriate place to declare the *shehada*. It is hard to imagine the fans at an English football match doing the same. The support groups that accompanied the contests seemed rather organised in a top-down way, as if the authorities had sponsored uniforms, as in East Africa when there is a presidential visit and the women are all kitted out to dance for him.

In Kordofan I had witnessed a very different dance among the Nubans. There, the male dancers wore grass raffia skirts with bells made from tins filled with pebbles hanging from their ankles. The movement of the feet was the music of the dance, too upbeat to be called shuffling, the shaking of the pebbles sounding quite dynamic when punctuated with blasts from a whistle. On each male dancer's head were horns, tied on to the head with white fabric, rather like a cartoon bandage when someone has toothache. The muslin cloth hung down behind like that of a damsel in an Arthurian legend, and cowries were suspended from the head over the face.

On one arm a dancer had a sheathed dagger, on the other a bundle of amulets. In one hand he carried a bell and in the other a handkerchief to wipe away the sweat, for the heat was intense. The women wore

Female supporters

he seemed not just a popular winner at a sports event but, with his strength matched by his gentle manner, I could see that this man was loved by those around him. I think now of the poet, who, in answer to the question of what he wanted from life, wrote:

To call myself beloved, to feel myself beloved on the earth.[5]

But Kerubino, although he had just basked in the warmth of the crowd, wanted to throw it all in. He claimed he was going to travel within a week but he wasn't going to do the usual Sudanese thing and work in the Gulf. It was Europe that he wanted; he would travel to Egypt and then Turkey and then Greece. As we walked to the *suq*, the evening darkening as we passed through the crowds, he threw his arm over my shoulder in that unconscious way that they do. I wasn't exactly enthusiastic about his plans, telling him that one of the lads from the Gezira who sell falafel sandwiches opposite my workplace, dropping balls of crushed chickpeas day after day into a pan of sizzling fat, had had the same dream. He had made it to Greece, smuggled in on a boat as part of the human trafficking that goes on, but had found no work, returning broke to fry falafel again on the pavement.

beautiful *tobes* and stood straight, moving in a very controlled way, while others gave themselves up to the dance. One of the dancers moved his head like a bull and feigned a rush at one of the women.

That's how it was in Kordofan. Here in *Suq Sitta*, by sunset, with the sun a hazy disc dipping below the fading fabric of the enclosure, it is all over. Without actually waiting for the referee's final whistle, spectators themselves often call the contest to an end by swarming onto the pitch, leaving the authorities as impotent onlookers. On this occasion, crowds gathered around Kerubino and myself, the *khawaja* as much an attraction as the local hero. Intermingling can have its hazards: one wrestler grabbed me by the thigh and made as if to raise me skywards to the delight of the bystanders. I feared less for myself than for my vari-focals.

As we moved away from the crowds for tea in the *suq*, Kerubino said he had something to tell me. To me at that moment

Dancer in Cadougleh, Kordofan

Jubilant spectators

We sat at the tea seller's in the street outside the shop where Kerubino makes a living selling mobile phones, an occupation difficult to reconcile with anyone who might wish to cast him in the role of 'noble savage' perhaps! Kerubino, having bought my tea, would have none himself; he drinks only milk or fresh fruit juice. The others explained.

'His strength is *rahma* – something given by God in his mercy.' And indeed there didn't seem to be a need to improve on what God had given; the Sudanese approach to training was not to work out in the gym, but to enjoy languid days preserving energy and eating well, with many an hour spent reclining in bed.

To my surprise, in the *suq* I was introduced to another wrestler, someone who did not have the typically Nuban stocky build. A gold cross on a chain fell around his neck. Angelo was from Rumbek, the Dinka heartlands of Sudan. Dinka and wrestler were for me an unusual collocation.

'You don't have wrestling in Rumbek, do you?'

'I grew up here in Khartoum! I learned to wrestle here!' It seemed to me that at least one Dinka in Khartoum had absorbed an essentially Nuban tradition, but the Dinka apparently have their own contests too.

I sat sipping the milky tea that is traditionally drunk after sunset. Around me the fare-collectors called from

their minibuses, beckoning passengers to Khartoum and Bahari, the milling crowds lit by the stark bulbs of the food stalls. It seemed a far cry from the sterile middle-class life of suburbia.

'And what's this *suq* called?'

'Unity Market. Everyone is here, and we all live as one!'

Indeed there seemed to be a lot of cultural fusion. And I had been wrong in thinking that wrestling belonged only to Nuban culture. Months later, when I was travelling in Kordofan, I chatted with a fellow guest in the *laconda* who traded in the powdery substance found within the pods of the baobab that is used to make a refreshing drink. He had lived among the Baggarah and Nubans in a mountain village, but was from a different ethnic group. He said that his tribe did not wrestle for a simple reason.

'Those Nubans and Baggarah wrestle because they have milk!'

Years ago in Kordofan, I had seen those pastoralists, the Baggarah, move with their camel trains in search of grazing, the women perched in the woven *beit* or shelter on the camel as the men walked. But I hadn't clicked here in the wrestling arena, when chatting to Sudani and his brother Kosti Bridge and others in the opposing team, that they were not Nuban. They were lighter skinned than the Nubans and were nomadic

'Arabs'. There was even one tubby wrestler, lacking in grace but not in perseverance, whom I heard came from Darfur. Perhaps the commentator was right in calling it 'Sudanese wrestling' after all.

I was enjoying Unity *Suq* and the ambience of the crowded market, but Kerubino, despite being the greatest Nuban wrestler of his day, wanted none of it. His one desire was to leave Sudan, but now there was a slight change to his itinerary; he would travel to Cairo and then to Turkey and then to Australia.

I could relate to how he felt; in Belfast in the eighties I had desperately wanted to leave, pacing the back room of a terraced house as I longed for other shores. Throwing in my job in a respectable school, I abandoned the life I knew for a volunteer's post in Africa. Teaching in a school at the desolately beautiful tip of an island in Lake Malawi had brought relief. Why should I try to deny to Kerubino what I had enjoyed myself?

What future was there for Kerubino in Sudan? Other Sudanese do not much respect the Nubans or their culture and much prefer the shenanigans of wrestling on satellite TV, especially the red-haired Irish World Wrestling Entertainment (WWE) wrestler Sheamus O'Shaunessy. Responding to the sight of almost naked white flesh, his fans tell me approvingly that Sheamus is 'as white as mayonnaise'. Sheamus is big in Sudan.

One day, as I set off for a short hike in South Kordofan, I was met with cries of '*khawaja, khawaja!*' from the kids, but calls of '*Shaaaayms, Shaaaayms!*' Sheamus is more of a celebrity than the traditional wrestlers.

Was the arrival of Sheamus in Sudan going to mark the end of traditions that go back to the time of the Pharaohs, whose tombs portray contests with wrestlers from the land of Nubia paying tribute to their Egyptian conquerors? The wrestlers' features in the friezes are very much African; indeed, one inscription refers to the defeat of the 'kinky-haired' ones.[6] There are those, perhaps fancifully, who argue for cultural continuity between the ancient Nubians and the Nuba people of Kordofan.[7] Is the traditional and authentic now to be replaced by the globally commercial and fake?

Others watched as I interrogated Sudan's champion wrestler.

'And what job will you do?'

'I'll box.' I was sceptical.

'Box? Do you think you can just move across from wrestling today to boxing tomorrow?'

'I'll do any work.' I believed him. But without a word of English and with even Arabic as a second language, who would employ Kerubino? The Nubans themselves speak a number of different languages with no one language to unite them.

'And where's Australia?' I asked. Sudan's champion wrestler was truly thrown by this question.

I went back to my stint of teaching in Juba. On returning to Khartoum, I phoned, but Kerubino's mobile was no longer in use. In the restaurant near work, one of the men breakfasting told me that he had left for Egypt. I went to *Suq Sitta* again and they confirmed that he had gone along with a bunch of others.

I didn't care for Nuban wrestling the same way after Kerubino's departure.

NOTES

1 Rodger, George, *Village of the Nubas* (Phaidon Press, 1999) p.ii

2 Ibid. p.9

3 Ibid. p.93

4 Ibid. p.93

5 Carver, Raymond, 'Late Fragment', *A New Path to the Waterfall* (Atlantic Monthly Press, 1989)

6 Carroll, Scott, 'Wrestling in Ancient Nubia', *Journal of Sport History*, Vol. 15: No. 2 (Los Angeles: Summer 1988), wysinger.homestead.com/nubiansport.html

7 Ibid.

CHAPTER FOUR

NEW SUDAN?

New Sudan had arrived. Or perhaps it would be more accurate to say, as the plane touched down on the runway at Rumbek, the main town in the lands of the Dinka, that I had arrived in New Sudan.

The Comprehensive Peace Agreement (CPA) had been signed in Kenya in 2005 by the Sudanese Vice-President Ali Osman Taha and Dr John Garang, the leader of the SPLA. A settlement had finally been reached between the rebels, mostly from the South, fighting for a New Sudan, and the Khartoum regime. Two decades of civil war had ended. The CPA formed the basis for a radical restructuring not just of the South but of all Sudan, from the legal system to the armed forces to the sharing of natural resources. But before the New Sudan could be delivered, Garang died in a helicopter crash and there were ethnic clashes in Khartoum.

When I arrived in Rumbek in 2006, the country was enjoying the interim period before the referendum in 2011 when Southerners would vote for either a 'united' Sudan that was one country, or for an independent South Sudan.

I arrived at a time of reconstruction. It was not just that the Gravy Train were going back and forth about their business, or the airport now had a customs office with an official asking if I had any books for him. Things were still quite basic, but essential structures were beginning to be put in place.

The reputation of the Dinka went before them. I had known them a little in Khartoum when I went occasionally to an illegal drinking den with sacking over a framework for shade on the shores of the Nile, out in the shanty towns, and invariably the Dinka would be there. I had also seen them in the streets of Khartoum, utterly marginalized, displaced within their own country, working on the building sites as casual labourers, perhaps eyed with suspicion. I sometimes thought of how the Irish had traditionally lived in London. They spoke an Arabic that *was* worse than my own and was much mocked by the Northerners, who of course could not speak a word of Dinka. When the day's work was done they bussed it back to the shanty towns or slept in the half-built concrete buildings that were very much part of the Khartoum landscape. They were constructing the city but had little part of it.

Now, in Rumbek, I found the Dinka in their own element. I was with them in their home territory, among their lush pastures and cattle, not by some black-market stall or squatting in some never-to-be-completed multi-storey.

I came to Rumbek during the rains, and I don't think I have ever seen a place so green, so lush as Rumbek at that time. It was said that with the civil war people had forgotten how to cultivate because so much of the land had been mined, but by the roadside the land was now thick with maize growing taller by the day. The fields were carelessly planted – in fact they were not so much fields as patches of maize with groundnuts spreading below the luxuriant leaves, but they were being farmed nevertheless. Land that had not been tilled in decades was now yielding a crop.

The thatched *tukkuls* that had been neglected during the war years were now being rebuilt or re-roofed with the grass that had sprung in the rains. By the roadside in the warm morning light villagers sat under the trees chatting affably, the elders seated on plastic chairs, for civilisation was now making its presence felt, with the younger men seated on the ground beneath the shading trees.

Already people who had fled during the war were returning home. In Malakal I had seen the great barges crammed with the displaced by the banks of the Nile, and from my classroom I had heard the river horns sounding out to warn the last lingering tea drinkers that their boat was about to leave, passing upriver through islands of floating water hyacinths for Juba and 'home'. What 'home' might mean after an absence of a decade or two was anyone's guess. For some, 'home' was a place they had never been to: some 'returning Southerners' had lived all their lives in the North.

In Rumbek in those days you could feel a lightness in the air, a delight in living, whether it was the abundance of the rains or the promise of a lasting peace. There were other signs of a returning normality: the *suqs* now had an affable buzz, with men and women gathering under the great tree that formed the heart of the tobacco market. The air was pungent with the cones of locally grown tobacco that were displayed on the stalls, and men from the cattle camps would sample some of the weed in the palm of their hands. It seemed all leisurely conversation, an endless series of greetings and, for some, sweet tea under the shade of a tree. I had expected aggro and attitude, but I was met with amused laughter. Here was a country with a chance to start afresh. I did, however, wonder a little how the New Sudan would be different from the old one I had known in the late-eighties in Khartoum.

I would be part of the reconstruction: South Sudan must have a civil service and I would be teaching essential skills to the civil servants of the Government of South Sudan, people who had maybe a year or two of secondary education, for their schooling had often been in the bush or in camps beyond Sudan's borders, and now made up the civil service of Lakes State. Essentially, men who were used to a guerrilla lifestyle would now have to settle down to an office job, even if their formal education was minimal. And they had fought without pay; one of my trainees missed the first couple of days of training as he was paying his men the first salaries they had received in over a decade.

Once, in Wau, I came across one of my trainees sitting by the riverbank revising for his secondary school exams. Khawaja — for that was his name — and his classmates would sit back with their books on the grassy bank and try and commit as much as possible to memory, for that

Portrait taken on the road to work

is what education here is all about: passive memorization. The history Khawaja was learning from his Sudanese text book must have been a bit hard to swallow given what he had witnessed in the war: he was committing to memory the wonders of Arab civilisation and the Ummayads. In contrast, in Dinka traditions the arrival of the Arab forces of the Khalifa Abdullahi is referred to as the time when the world was spoiled.[1]

I was part of that exclusive group 'the international community', who were now present in strength. There were so many NGOs in the area a teacher could do an Alphabet Beginners course just from the names of the 'non-governmental' organisations who were present: OXFAM, WORLD VISION, MAG... They were taking on the roles that were normally those of a government, perhaps thus allowing a government to renege on its civil responsibilities.

Like the other expats I lived in an ensuite tent in a camp near the runway. I even had a contingency fund of a wad of dollars in case a flight to Nairobi became suddenly desirable. The camp was run by a Kenyan safari company, and staying there, I imagine, was like being on safari but without the wildlife; the wild game of South Sudan had fled two opposing armies or fled across national boundaries in search of sanctuary elsewhere. But already there was talk that the displaced wild game was returning.

The camp was a little First World enclave in the African bush with the liquid sounds of the hornbills spilling through the trees and someone coming to make the bed in the morning. Residents could even email or check stocks and shares from their tents, and with 24-hour electricity it certainly wasn't camping as I had known it in the scouts. Nor was I encountering Africa as I had done as a volunteer in my youth, teaching in a basic government school at the tip of an island in Lake Malawi; expats here lived at a considerable remove.

The heart of the Rumbek campsite was, of course, the bar, and in the warmth of the evening we would be served up barbecued pork or pasta by Kenyan chefs in uniforms. The Gravy Train had its own separate dining place, but I was getting a sense of how the other half lived. Although we were surrounded by cattle and pastoralists, even the meat was flown in from Nairobi. I suppose that was all part of promoting sustainable living, but it could also have been that our neighbours, the greatest cattle herders of the continent, have too much reverence for their cattle just to sell them for meat. After dinner I would sit around the bar with the Kenyans, enjoying the cordiality of fellow drinkers, glad not to be drinking yet another cup of sugary tea under a tree in Khartoum.

After dry Khartoum, the normal freedoms of life were simply a relief. It was as if a little bit of Mombasa had been transferred to Sudan, but without the beach. Even the currency was Kenyan shillings and the Kenyans had a sound business sense. When it came to catering, the Hilton in Khartoum could not have done a better job.

Some of the expats had lived in the camp for months, but had never once made it into town a couple of miles away to nip into the grocers' shops with their shelves of soap and tinned food and Ugandan whisky. Their only sense of Rumbek was the drive between the camp and their office on the outskirts. The town was out of bounds for some; it wasn't safe, I was told, to leave the car.

The Gravy Train was there in the camp in force as part of the monitoring of the peace agreement, but I did wonder if they ever got out of their vehicles. How could you keep the peace but not know how to say hello to someone in their language? And it wasn't difficult to learn the greetings in Dinka. I would walk or cycle into work through a landscape of lush palms and strangling figs and by the time I arrived at the compound where I taught I'd have greeted maybe 50 people on the way, the villagers asking with mock horror, 'But where is your car?' for it was unthinkable that a *khawaja* should be walking.

Informal language lessons were also taking place in the camp. In the morning, the International Community would gather over breakfast and the buzzwords of the aid industry could be heard over pancakes and bacon: ' ... sustainability ... transparency ... project objectives ... gender balance ... capacity building... ' It was essential to sprinkle anything said about development with a liberal dash of such words. Giving language training to the civil servants I felt at times that all I was doing was teaching people to repeat the lingo of development, rather than rationalize the concepts the words were used to express, or even challenge them.

Just outside the camp's electrified fence it was a different story, with a few *tukuls* near the gates where local people gathered for tea amid the usual squalor of half-naked kids and Kalashnikovs set against the wall of the hut. Across the way, drivers from Uganda and their teams would sit under the trees maintaining the lorries they had driven for maybe two weeks to deliver sorghum or the like to the relief programmes. The Ugandan crews would be genial enough as they cooked some stew under a tree as I crossed the gates to the camp where I ate so well that I was putting on weight. Not everyone, however, had it so good; I met one of the crew out with a catapult hoping to shoot a bird to eat with his corn meal. Outside the camp, beyond the pale if you will, there seemed to be an endless gathering of men sitting indolently under the trees, and not without reason. Just as we had our Pilsner lager at the bar, the villagers, too, had their refreshments.

By tradition, the Dinka are not so much cultivators like the Nuba, but pastoralists leading a nomadic life. Traditionally, they have had their more permanent settlements in the savannah lands, with the young migrating to the dry season camps and fresh pastures near the tributaries of the White Nile when the swamps dry out. The war totally disrupted those established patterns of transhumance and grain was given as essential food aid.

In the long term, grain given as aid has hardly stimulated the desire to cultivate, but I suppose it keeps the US farmers and voters happy and it does have its uses. The Dinka have traditionally enjoyed a local brew from sorghum, a nourishing intoxication like a light grainy porridge. It's a good public relations exercise, with the locals enjoying a kind of extended Happy Hour that lasted through to the softening light of dusk, when I would make sure that I was back within the security of the electrified fence to enjoy a lager at the bar.

Early in the morning, I'd be on my way into town, trying out some of the words I had learnt. One of the first phrases I knew was *Chalai di?* And when I asked someone their name I would get an answer like 'The bull with the spots' or 'Rain', and I assumed he had been born in the time of rain. This was a welcome change from the monocultures of the world religions, where in one part of Sudan a boy is likely to be called Ahmed or Abdullah, and in the other, Peter or John seem about the only current options. Girls are given names such as Rose and Grace, names that died out elsewhere generations ago. In contrast, African traditions show an incredible wealth of names. When I was a volunteer in Malawi, one of my best students had been called Hopeless because all the siblings that had preceded him had died young.

One of the trainees told me that his name was The Bull, but looking back on it now his answer must surely have been more specific than that. I was beginning to get a sense of things, and asked if the Dinka gave their cattle names too. I got the impression that men and cattle shared the same names: a name could be that of a young man wearing an earring, or it could describe the colours of a bull passed on the road. I asked one man why he had been given his name.

'It's after the bull that my father gave to my mother's family when they got married.'

'As a dowry?'

'Yes, but along with other cattle and goats.'

'And did they keep the bull?'

'It was slain in the ceremony.'

'The wedding ceremony?'

'Yes. And I was given this name to remember that bull.' There's something appealing about the first born from the marriage being named after the very bull that was sacrificed in the ceremony. The Dinka are not great meat eaters; cattle are sacrificed to mark an occasion, not just butchered for meat. The bull would have been ritually served up to the guests, but it was commemorated in the name of the first son born after the ceremony in which it was slain.

After initiation, a young man will have his own personal ox, and he will have a second name reflecting the colours of the ox with which he is linked. A man called Mabior will have a white ox, for that is what such an ox is called; Malual will have been named after his red-brown ox. Majok could be a black and white ox or the young man proudly walking with it, or the black and white beads worn around his neck. He will compose songs about his ox; he is more likely to sing about the ox that accompanies him than about the girl he is to marry. Wyndham, with his usual gentle humour, wrote about what is dear to Dinka hearts: 'When they sing a love-song, it is about a cow

or a bull.'² Lines from a traditional poem translated by Francis Mading Deng reflect this, where the dark brown body which the young man celebrates is that of his ox, an ox that walks gingerly, placing its feet 'like a girl wearing coils on her legs'.³

ARMS AND THE MAN

It is not just cattle that are slain. One night, I awoke in the tent to hear extensive gunfire, as if a nearby open-air cinema were playing the soundtrack too loud; the Dinka were at it again. They are, after all, the Warriors of the White Nile, and they have a long tradition of cattle raids. That is what life is about: cattle. However, when a Kalashnikov is now the essential fashion accessory – who would be seen grazing the cattle without one? – the stakes are upped more than a little.

There was a certain volatility to it all. As a teacher in Sudan, I am used to excuses from latecomers to class, but in Rumbek it was different: a civil servant turned up late and explained that his uncle had been shot; it had taken six hours to get him to the hospital. Another arrived late and told me that his neighbours had beaten him with a stick; in the case of this individual, I empathized with the neighbours. I don't know whether or not the men with sticks had been a girl's irate brothers. When a suitor negotiates with the bride's family the number of cattle to go to her family as dowry, disagreements are usually settled through a kind of bargaining. Given that there is apparently a taboo on naming the precise number of cattle, for that would invite calamity, it is hard to imagine how such bargaining is done. But an unwelcome suitor might meet the girl's brothers carrying sticks or worse.

If a man doesn't have the requisite cattle there are two options. One is to 'elope' with a girl, and I suspect the word here is a euphemism; we are not talking of Shylock's daughter stepping onto a gondola one moonlit night with her beloved. Girls in Dinka culture are a source of wealth. Samuel Baker contrasted the expense of bringing up girls in Victorian England with the wealth that girls brought to a family in the South of Sudan, writing that '....a large family is a source of wealth: the girls bring the cows, and the boys milk them.'[4] Since the girl's relatives would miss out on the cattle that would be given as dowry, conflict is the likely result of 'elopement'. The other option is a cattle raid, which might bring the requisite dowry and do a lot for a young man's reputation. But the stakes have been upped with all the weaponry obtained in the war, and the principal arms nowadays are not spears but Kalashnikovs.

To an outsider, marriage among the Dinka is not a particularly romantic matter. My trainees themselves would joke about it: how such and such a woman, tall and beautiful, and with certain teeth appropriately shaped would bring a lot of cows when she married. It seemed to me sometimes that it was not that cows were a means to marriage, but marriage the means to gain more cows.

Among the Dinka, the norms of relationships are very different from those of the 'Arab' Sudanese. Among Northerners, marrying a cousin is a norm; with the Dinka, marrying a cousin would not only be seen as incest but a rather pointless exercise for the family would acquire no cattle in the process. Even the dead can in a sense 'marry'. Just before the referendum, I was teaching English to a group of lawyers in Juba. We focussed on texts about legal rights and the family in the UK, and some rather removed matters like intellectual property law, but the trainees also presented matters related to their own customary law. And so I learnt that among the Dinka, if a man dies single a brother will marry on his behalf and the children will bear the dead man's name. Or, if the deceased was married, one of his relatives will marry his widow and have children on the dead man's behalf; a tradition not far from some Old Testament practices.

One of the courses taught to the civil servants was conflict resolution in the workplace, but I wondered what I could teach the trainees on such a subject; they knew a lot more about conflict than I could imagine. Even when men from one Dinka clan raid another, the ramifications for peace are enormous.

The Southern Sudanese are no more one ethnic group than Europeans and there has been a long tradition of conflict among the tribes of the South. Travelling through Sudan between 1886 and 1871, the German naturalist Georg Schweinfurth wrote of the Nuer, living between the tributaries of the White Nile, as hemmed in by hostile neighbours.[5] The 'hostile neighbours' does not just refer to the northern 'Arabs'; in the civil war, ethnic groups like the Nuer have switched sides, sometimes being part of the SPLA against the Khartoum regime, sometimes fighting with the regime against the SPLA dominated by their traditional enemies, the Dinka.

I didn't have to go far in Rumbek to see some of the casualties of conflict; just a few minutes from the camp, Boum sat in his wheelchair, an arm and a leg amputated after 'a local skirmish'. And then there was Ox at the compound where we held the course, with one leg amputated from a war injury. His HIV-awareness T-shirt warned of a new enemy.

Dinka woman met on the road, Rumbek

As I walked into work, all around there would be military-style parades. I think some were the new prison officers being drilled carrying imitation wooden guns as part of their training. Those young men and women parading outside the village huts under their leader's vigilant eye were, I think, SPLA recruits. And without doubt, the lorry loads of troops outside the compound were SPLA being transferred to a new posting.

But this was now 'post-conflict'. The key military now held the main civilian posts. But how could their leadership style change from a military one to a style appropriate to the civil service or a hospital? Were the skills that made a guerrilla leader successful in the bush transferable to the local council? Even after all my years in the Middle East, with its blend of khaki and kitsch, I had never come across such a militarized society. Could guerrilla leaders become the leaders of a democratic society?

That week, there were substantial 'cattle raids' and up to 60 citizens on the outskirts of Rumbek were killed. But it would be wrong to suggest that Rumbek was without law and order. Once, when cycling into town, I just nipped left on my bicycle rather than go all the way around the roundabout. An eagle-eyed traffic policeman spotted my misdemeanour and summoned me to explain my disregard for the law. It took all my negotiating skills to talk my way out of an on-the-spot fine and Mr Ruben Deng and I eventually parted on good terms. It was heart-warming to see law and order being enforced in town, even if it was only on the one *khawaja* riding a bicycle.

A SENSE OF BEAUTY

Some of the men had a distinctive beauty, a slimness of form and finely chiselled facial features that belied their warring traditions. The young men of the cattle camps often had an almost feminine, though not effeminate, attractiveness, which they would set off with an ear-ring or a necklace of black and white beads. The jewel in the crown would be the *nok*, a little tuft of ostrich feathers rising above the head. Perhaps there was a certain vanity, but the hairstyles seem to have diminished since the 1930s when Wyndham observed warriors in three-foot high busbies of black ostrich plumes.

One problem that traders arriving in the Dinka lands faced was the Dinka disregard for items such as cloth brought for bartering. They attached little value to possessions, even clothes, and traders met an insurmountable barrier, for with the Dinka disdain for clothing they could not be induced to part with their cattle for anything they were offering.

Fashions have somewhat changed since Wyndham's visit to Bahr-el-Ghazal, when there seemed to be only one rule for male dress, which might be the equivalent of a western ostentatious display of wealth: 'There is one convention that these Dinka men follow rigidly; whatever part of their body they may choose to cover, it is not that part which you would most expect.'[6] A sense of shame of the body was not a natural thing among the Dinka and had to be cultivated by the missionaries and Muslim believers.

Why would a Dinka male cover himself? Traditionally, any kind of clothing was for women. Observing Dinka notions of propriety, Schweinfurth wrote that it was thought unmanly for a male to wear any kind of clothing. The botanist kept his clothes on and the Dinka came to a logical conclusion, ironically referring to him as the Turkish lady.[7]

Schweinfurth is not the only male foreigner in Sudan to have been addressed in the feminine form. To this day in Blue Nile State, any Chinese man walking in the market is addressed as 'my friend', the Chinese male blissfully unaware that, possibly because of his lack of moustache or beard, he is being addressed in the feminine form, *saddiqa*.

In the cattle camps these days, the young men usually wear a simple pinafore not unlike a *jelabiyah*, but with a hemline at the knees. The kids, however, walk around

Dinka youth with ostrich feathers in his cap, Rumbek

At a cattle camp near Rumbek town

stark naked. One of my trainees, now appropriately dressed as a civil servant, admitted to never having worn any clothes until he was 13 years old, when he had started primary school. He had had one year of secondary school before entering his profession.

Ornamentation, not surprisingly, relates to cattle. The Dinka are very adept at recycling; cow dung is burnt in the evenings to ward off the gathering insects and the ash is used to cover the entire body, both as a mosquito repellent and as decoration. Cow urine is a disinfectant used not only to wash the dishes or the gourds but also to dye the hair.

These traditions would be common to the Shilluk and Nuer as well. In his 1930s visit, Wyndham observed the beauty of the porters of the Nile with an artist's sensitivity: 'They were astonishingly beautiful as they moved among the pools of lamplight, their velvet-dark bodies incredibly tall and slender, their long hair blond.'[8] Had the artist smoked something grown on the banks of the Nile? With typical mischief, Wyndham then undermines his own lyricism: 'So what matter that their hair was dyed with cow-piss?'

Those are the traditions. The young man about town nowadays, however, might go for an NGO shirt advertising a Measles Vaccination Campaign, or an HIV T-shirt with the slogan 'Keeping the Promise',

Burning cow dung to ward off insects in the evenings

which would give a certain street cred. How a young man is to 'keep the promise' and embrace celibacy until he has enough cattle has never been explained to me.

I suppose the ultimate signs of maleness were the tribal markings; they give the men a certain magnificence, the face itself a work of art. As far as I know, the Dinka of Rumbek don't practise circumcision; instead, they cut the forehead of a boy as he approaches manhood. The initiation markings signal that a boy has moved from being a boy who could be ordered about at anyone's command to being officially an adult.

I suppose the markings are akin to circumcision. I saw it once among the Maasai in Kenya. The young men were escorted into the village gloriously naked, the occasion marked by head-dresses of feathers, dancing and libations of milk poured over the body flowing on to the soil, the initiate silently undergoing the cut of the knife. As among the Maasai, the Dinka boy who cried out under the cut of the knife might find himself stigmatized.

The scars are deep. Having lived among the Dinka with the photographer Sarah Errington in 1976, John Ryle was given a good insight into Dinka traditions by a doctor when he was shown a skeleton in Rumbek hospital. The markings had not been skin-deep; on the upper part of the skull, the bone itself was furrowed by six distinct grooves. [9]

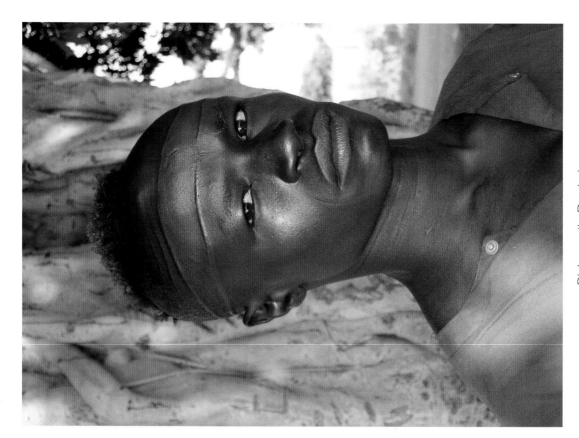

Dinka youth, Rumbek

Another kind of marking, I was told, is a horizontal cut on the arm, apparently a form of tally, a notch for each man killed in battle. Or so my trainees told me, but I suspect they were pulling the *khawaja's* leg in this case. I did a quick inspection in class but to no avail; even in Rumbek it's hardly one of the criteria for being a civil servant.

Teeth are also an area where a Dinka sense of beauty might differ from others'. The males often have the middle teeth of the lower jaw removed, an endurance of pain I thought of as signalling 'manliness' until I found that some of the women have theirs removed too. More commonly, in contrast to the pressure teenagers in the west endure to wear a brace to keep everything uniformly even, a woman's teeth might be made to protrude from the lips to great effect. Samuel Baker records how a woman of the Latookas made some recommendations as to how Florence might make herself more attractive:

She said that my wife would be much improved if she would extract her four front teeth from the lower jaw and wear the red ointment on her hair, according to the fashion of the country.[10]

Beauty is most definitely in the eye of the beholder; the western obsession with rings in navels and tongues might seem equally bizarre to the Dinka.

The essential accoutrement for a man was a gun, but he might also carry a clay pipe or a radio playing music as he walked. The women walking single file along the path, however, would always be carrying something more substantial: a water pot, a baby, a massive pile of firewood. It was not just a matter of men travelling light; it seemed that the only possessions that were valued by the Dinka were their cattle but even so, I doubt if any Dinka would see himself as 'owning' cattle. The relationship went far beyond that.

It was a world of machismo with Shaggy, Nelly and 50 Cent as entertainment and role models and Dinka singers themselves aspiring to rap. Somewhere, the values of Dinka warriors in Rumbek and New York street gangs must overlap. I thought the Kalashnikov effect a little undermined, however, when the arms bearer on the motorbike also had his nails painted with red nail varnish. It was a relief walking back from work one day to come across two women doing each other's hair in the shade by one of the huts.

Pipe-smoker, Rumbek

A world of machismo

How women travel, Wau

A SENSE OF BEAUTY: PART TWO

The cattle had an incredible beauty that was not lost even on me; perhaps it was their sandy colour, or the way some of them had horns shaped with a knife by those who cared for them, just as some ancient Egyptian tombs are decorated with images of cattle with shaped horns. The Dinka lovingly bend the horns of their cattle, and even as he dances a man will hold up his arms curved above his head in imitation of shapely horns, not so much a case of man imitating art, as man empathizing with his cattle: he is himself like an ox.

The Dinka see the world through the colours of their cattle. Where Ireland has the dull monoculture of the Friesian, mere black and white, grazing in mono-fields of phosphate-induced green, the cattle of the savannah show incredible variety and the Dinka language has developed a wealth of vocabulary to describe colours and shades. They have over 100 different colour combinations for describing their cattle. If the Irish, according to a dreadful sentimental song, could once see 100 shades of green, then the Dinka can see 100 hues of the cattle grazing in the pastures. The anthropologist Godfrey Lienhardt writes that Dinka 'perception of colour, light, and shade in the world around them is ... inextricably connected with their recognition of colour configurations in their cattle.'[11] The blues of the sky

and rivers, however, also seemed to me reflected in the vibrant colours of their clothes.

Though renowned as warriors, the Dinka are essentially pastoralists, moving seasonally in search of the fresh pastures that the rains bring. There is also the daily movement in search of grazing; as I walked home from work, some child aged about 12 would be guiding the cattle home from the pastures. At such an age my only responsibility had been my books and pencil case; a Dinka child, however, might be answerable for the entire wealth of the family, driving the herd out to the pastures after the morning milking. Cattle are more valued than education: the most talented boys care for the cows; the less gifted are sent to school.

As the light softened in the afternoon, I would find myself riding on my bicycle through a herd of cows, which moved gently aside to let me pass, the boy a little startled to see a *khawaja* at such close distance. It was strange to find cattle so docile among people with a reputation for aggression. At home I wouldn't set foot in a field with a bull, but here I would walk inches from some bull's horns, or wheel my bike a foot from the head, neither the bull nor myself overly concerned. I suppose the same principle applied to more than just cattle; things I accepted as norms abroad would have terrified me at home.

The cattle camp I visited with one of my trainees was about an hour's cycle from town. Even that was a sign of recovery; in the war years, I heard, no one would have brought their cattle so close to the main settlements, but now I was able to come across a traditional way of life just a few kilometres from class. On approaching the camp there was the mooing of cattle. Some young lad with a Kalashnikov was guarding it all while a warrior in a pinafore walked by with his bull. And then the children came running out, as curious about me as I was about their way of life.

An encounter on the road

The aesthetics of cattle

At the cattle market, Wau

Traditionally, it would be fair to say that without cattle a Dinka is seen as a nobody, and the relationship between the Dinka and their cattle goes beyond mere material considerations like milk yield. But the Dinka do have their ways to increase yield, although it does not involve playing Mozart to bovine ears. Back in the 1930s, Wyndham saw a Dinka lad with his face submerged in the rear of a cow, blowing into its backside 'as if trying to inflate an air-mattress with a broken valve'.[12] He was observing the standard method among the Dinka of trying to get a barren cow to yield milk. It is still practised today.

The docility of the cattle has something to do with the closeness between the Dinka and their animals, and the relationship is a very physical one. I would see a man dusting his bull down with ash to protect and beautify it, just as a resident of the suburbs might polish the car at the weekend. He would pat and massage the bull with wood ash, the dust rising like talcum powder in the air. A man's intimacy with his bull would be seen in his massaging its erogenous zones and I do not mean the genitals alone. It is not just the men who appreciate the beauty of cattle. Lienhardt writes that he was told by a Dinka girl that she would prefer to marry a somewhat ugly young man with a fine ox rather than a handsome man with an indifferent ox.[13] It is the cattle that bring status.

At the cattle market, Wau

AID AGAIN

Sometimes my attempts at Dinka would be met with an outstretched hand and a couple of words of debased Arabic as the speaker demanded money. It was ridiculous to see some strapping warrior half a metre taller than myself point to his stomach and speak of hunger on seeing a *khawaja*. It was even more pathetic to see some elderly man, in perfect health, go through some pantomime of appealing for food. On being given short shrift by myself, gaining more middle-aged spread on three good meals a day at the camp, the response was as often as not good-natured laughter. Clearly people were just trying it on.

It's one thing to supply schools with breakfast so the children have something in their stomachs to get them through the school day, but now that the maize is growing tall and the land is being cleared of mines, maybe it's time to question the desirability of handouts. In the end, maybe it's a matter of self-interest: the cultivation of a dependency culture, as opposed to encouraging the cultivation of fields, keeps a lot of 'the international community' in a job.

Conflict keeps many a westerner employed. In Sudan you have the situation where an embassy or government department will present its government as massively contributing to humanitarian relief; less publicised is their support for the military who

Cattle camp near Rumbek

Given that the relationship between the Dinka and their cattle goes way beyond mere material considerations, could it in some way be seen as spiritual? Cattle unite the clan in the sense that events that bind people together are celebrated with their sacrifice, but for Ryle it goes beyond even this. Cattle, as mankind's most precious possession, are the perfect sacrifice, linking humanity to the divine. When an animal is sacrificed it returns as a messenger to God.[14]

are creating the humanitarian crises in Darfur and Kordofan. With such empowering of the military, the humanitarian work will always be in demand.

With the hoped-for end of conflict, a lot of readjusting was being done. About town there were billboards showing the khaki-clad father standing by the mosquito-net-protected bedside of his child: the guerrilla fighter turned family man. That was not, however, the only adjustment that needed to be made. The guerrilla fighter was to be rewarded with his post of public servant and the military needed somehow to be demobilized, not just in terms of their clothing but in their thinking. That would take some doing.

I had witnessed it one morning at breakfast, not in Rumbek but in Wau. I had been staying in a modest lodge by the river with a simple dining room and bar. I had heard the place had once been a mess for British officers and it was now almost like a religious retreat in its simple aesthetics. Across from me, at another table, a civil servant was having breakfast. Unfortunately, the guest was served up a bad egg.

Others would pay for this mishap. First there was the public humiliation of the Kenyan waiter. Then the manager was called and an explanation demanded. Then, to cap it all, the irate official picked up his satellite phone and threatened military action! I saw it all myself, not in a comic episode of *Faulty Towers*, but over breakfast by the River Jur, a civil servant threatening military action because of a bad egg. It confirmed something I had suspected about life in the New Sudan: there are quite a few men now in safari suits throwing their weight around in public life. One of the lads guarding the rest-house in Darfur had a phrase for it: 'Those guys have got the power disease.'

This was not the only illness threatening us. On the trees in Rumbek there were posters pinned to the trunks, some in Juba Arabic – Arabic words, Latin script – promoting Aids awareness, while elsewhere a sign posted by some local 'doctor' advertised a dubious cure for Aids.

Posters abounded: one advertised an evangelical rally, its name, 'Sun after Rain', reflecting its external origins, for in Sudan it is the rains, not the sun, that are longed for. The public were invited to attend and have peace restored, health restored and even stolen possessions restored. I wondered if they could restore my bicycle, which had been stolen from under the noses of the guards at the camp.

I found myself wondering what kind of values the Dinka would now embrace. In the Victorian era, David Livingstone saw not aid but the combination of Christ and commerce as saving Africa, an alternative to the slave trade. The British nowadays seem to be going for the commerce, without Christ. 'Trade not Aid' goes the cliché, but the Americans seem to be going for the Livingstone solution.

The Kenyans at the camp seemed to have learned the lesson well, with the cashier at the bank giving his testimony of how he had been 'saved'. Having grown up in the north of Ireland the discourse of 'being saved' was one with which I was more than familiar, but now it had been transposed to the African bush. How did Dinka concepts of divinity transform into western evangelic portrayals of God? Having successfully fought off an invasive Islam, were the Dinka now to be 'saved' at some US-style rally instead? Would South Sudan TV soon be featuring telly-evangelists, appealing for a return to family values and a donation? And what about my role in this Americanization of Dinka life? Had I not myself delivered a day's training on customer care to civil servants, some of whom had survived years of warfare in the bush? Were the Warriors of the White Nile now to become client-orientated service providers and see their former guerrilla fighters as fellow customers? Would the Dinka fight future battles with a belief in customer care, the free market and a mid-year staff appraisal?

On my last morning in Rumbek, the women were out with their brooms sweeping the runway. Soon I would be on my way back to Khartoum, for that's

how it is: the 'expert' flies in, offers some utterly alien solution and flies out again. That morning, as I had my last walk along the road it seemed as if anyone I greeted just asked me for money. One man wearing shorts even asked me for trousers; did he expect me to take mine off and give them to him there and then?

Anyone working in the Aid Industry must surely question the appropriateness of what they are doing, although I know that NGOs like Oxfam deliver to the desperately needy and seriously tackle poverty at its roots. There are few nowadays who would hold up the old colonials or the missionaries as models for development, but I have seen the missionaries interacting with the poor, speaking the language, providing an education for the dispossessed.

I suppose what I had been doing in providing training for the civil servants in some way had its place in a kind of Great Game. I was one of the most minor players and I didn't really know what game was being played. Was the goal merely a functioning civil service within a unified Sudan? Or was the infrastructure being built for a separate state in the South, an oil-producing state that would provide the west with a source of fuel independent of the alienated Islamic world?

Was I witnessing a lasting peace? Or was it just an interlude during which oil revenues would be used to re-arm? Garang had wanted a New Sudan with the entire country reformed: that was his dream. Was the Southern leadership merely paying lip service to Garang's vision while creating its own separate state of South Sudan? Was this just a brief interlude until the referendum, when Southerners would secede and North and South, refreshed from the short interval, could set to with renewed vigour for another 50 years?

Even here, when I write of Khartoum and the South as opposing entities, it ignores the realities of the streets of the capital. Like that way of making tea in Egypt where it is all thrown in together, the tea leaves and the milk and the spices to be boiled together in one big pot, so Khartoum seemed to have drawn all Sudan to its streets. If Southerners were to vote for secession where would that leave the million and more Southerners in Khartoum? Marooned?

Just before I left Rumbek, I met a man walking along the road, barefoot and rather strangely decked out in a hat of hide and a kind of *jelabiyah*, but wearing a striped shirt that a man might wear to the office, except that this shirt was grubby. A young Dinka lad who was going off to sell cigarettes in the *suq* told me in his excellent primary school English that I had met a Spear Man. The Spear Man! This was the highest religious office among the Dinka, the Spear Man being the one who leads the sacrificial ceremonies. I had heard that he was the one to whom the tribe would turn if there was no rain. And his powers were apparently not only benign; he could not only divert misfortune, I was told, but also bring calamity on those who crossed him.

One of my trainees was the son of a Spear Man, but surely the two generations, the priest of the tribe and the state's civil servant, belonged to entirely different eras, if not ways of seeing the world. Did that young civil servant believe that his father had held the powers attributed to him? What place did the Spear Man now have among performance management courses, rap singers and evangelical rallies?

Lienhardt writes of the last days of the Master of the Fishing Spear and how, as his eyesight faded, he would call those close to him to prepare his grave. It was not an occasion of weeping but of rejoicing, with two great bulls being slaughtered and feasting and dancing, while the aged man was lowered alive on the skin of a sacrificed bull into his grave. And there he would lie for days, maybe amid the celebrations, speaking to the elders from his grave, prophesying, perhaps, until finally, when he no longer answered his people's calls, he was buried, not with earth but with the dung of the cattle that sustained their lives. Heaps of dung were thrown onto the grave, until the Master of the Fishing Spear was 'taken into the earth', his death affirming, as in some ancient Celtic rite, the continuity of the tribe.

Already by 1950 the authorities had all but brought such practices to an end. But what about today's Spear Man walking along the Rumbek road as the occasional Land-cruiser passed with its aid workers? Did he still have the respect of the English-speaking lad going off to sell cigarettes? Did he not feel redundant in the New Sudan?

I know that Orpheus playing the lyre at dawn did not cause the sun to rise, and I doubt if there are many civil servants in Lakes State who entirely believe in the values represented by the Spear Man. But as the World Food Programme plane flew from Rumbek back to Khartoum, I savoured the land below, a landscape so unlike the hedged-in fields of Ireland: vast plains with their occasional clusters of *tukkuls*; the boundless savannah lands through which the Dinka roamed, seeing the world through the colours of their cattle, migrating seasonally from settlement to river camp. I found myself wondering about that last encounter on the road: what would the new South be like, and what would replace the Spear Man and the beliefs that he once embodied?

NOTES

1 Ryle, John and Errington, Sara, *Warriors of the White Nile: The Dinka* (Time Life Books, 1982) p.28
2 Wyndham, op. cit. p.62
3 Beckwith, Carol and Fisher, Angela, *African Ceremonies, vol. 2* (Harry N. Abrams, Inc. New York, 1999) p.12
4 Baker, op. cit.
5 Schweinfurth, Georg, *The Heart of Africa: Three Years Travels and Adventures in the Unexplored Regions of Central Africa From 1868 to 1871* (Afro Am-Press, 1961) p.119
6 Wyndham, op. cit. p.83
7 Schweinfurth, op. cit. p.152
8 Wyndham, op. cit. p.45
9 Ryle and Errington, op. cit. p.142
10 Baker, op. cit.
11 Lienhardt, Godfrey, *Divinity and Experience* (Oxford Unity Press, 1961) pp.12–13
12 Wyndham, op. cit. p.101
13 Lienhardt, op. cit. p.18
14 Ryle and Errington, op. cit. p.89

CHAPTER FIVE

BENEATH THE HOLY MOUNTAINS

I pulled back the shutters of the dingy hotel room with its two single beds pushed together by the previous occupants to make one and the air-conditioning on throughout the cool night to dispel mosquitoes, and looked out over the flat roofs of Kassala. The wait for the permission to travel; the interminable delay as the bus filled up; the journey through plains dotted with acacia; the near accident at dusk with another vehicle: in the gentle light of early morning it all seemed worthwhile.

I gazed over the flat roofs of the town to take in the stark outline of the Taka Mountains, the morning sky rosy behind them. So utterly vertical were the *jebbels* of Kassala they could have been the mountains in some children's storybook where the hills pop up out of the page. They were sheer, grey, bald rock, but rock that would melt and soften according to the angle of the sun.

When the German–Russian explorer Wilhelm Junker stayed in Kassala in 1876 after trekking from Suakin, a leopard that had escaped from his host's menagerie strayed into his room. The plains in his day had been home to 'elephants, giraffes, buffaloes, antelopes and rhinoceros and ostrich'.[1] That diversity has all been lost, but the view of the mountains was essentially the same: 'Granite crags towering in picturesque disorder one above the other, the highest peaks piercing the clouds like the domes and spires of some gigantic minster.'[2] Less heavenly were the streets, characterized by 'sand, dirt and unsavoury smells penetrating everywhere'.[3]

Down in the street that day Kassala smelt of coffee and dust. Already an elderly man had his charcoal stove and cups displayed under a tree, but before I could have my first coffee of the day the first blind beggar and his boy were asking for alms. The town is not without its destitute. Kassala and its region are utterly marginalized.

Beyond the mountains was Eritrea. On arriving in Kassala it seemed as if I had already crossed some kind of border, for the town has a distinctly tribal feel. The main ethnic group in the region is the Beja, with the Hadendawa being the best-known Beja tribe. A fair proportion of its inhabitants are people for whom international borders make little sense but have a huge impact. Given the conflicts beyond its border, Kassala has hosted thousands upon thousands of refugees.

It is this distinct apartness that makes the town so appealing for travellers. The Hadendawa still come into town sporting hair-dos like those of 1970s soul groups and stand with their arms hanging casually over a stick resting on their shoulders. In the *suq*, you can still see someone selling a tanned leather sheath for a great two-edged sword.

But Kassala is not without its feminine side. Rashaida women sit on their hunkers in the street in luxuriant black and red dresses, their limbs bedecked with chunky silver jewellery. An Orientalist painter could not have exaggerated their exoticism, with a breast discreetly given to the baby. The men, vain to a man, wear white. I guess that even to the Sudanese, the Rashaida are exotic; they live apart, piling into the back of a pick-up in the late afternoon for their camp outside the town where they live with their

livestock. Their very accents reveal their strangeness: their Arabic is of the Hejaz.

To the citizens of the capital, the Hadendawa of Kassala are simply backward. As the labourers who cultivate the roundabout in Khartoum Two, irrigating the frangipani with all its creamy blooms put it, 'Those guys, they just spend the day drinking coffee. And all they carry with them is their coffee and the pot for making it in.' They would then spend the rest of the morning chatting under the neem tree with the tea lady, while the water trickled from the hosepipes on to parched roots.

When their work-mate from Kassala approached in his green overalls, slighter and leaner than themselves, they just addressed him as *ya Adarawb*! They might have been working together for years, but the Sudanese tend not to address someone from that tribe by name, they just call them by the generic name *Adarawb*, and deny that this is derogatory. *Adarawb*, I have heard, means red. This turned out to be one of the delights of Kassala for me. When a tribesman would involuntarily call out '*Ya khawaja*!' on seeing me pass by – just in case I did not know my identity in Sudan – I could instantly reply in a similar vein.

'What's up, *ya Adarawb*?'

The dress of the Hadendawa men is distinctive: a dark waistcoat over a tunic that hangs over very baggy

Rashaida man in a Suakin café

sirwal trousers that sometimes seem more ashen grey than white, over a metre in width, pulled tight with a drawstring. The essential fashion accessory, if not a sword, is a smooth narrow piece of wood, shaped like a boomerang but less curved, thrown in hunting or fighting. Unlike the boomerang, the *safarawq* does not return to the thrower, but then in expert hands there would be no need for a second throw: the victim is unlikely to know what hit it.

Arabic is very much a second language among the Hadendawa. Though dismissed as a *rutaana* by Arabic speakers, their language is one of the most ancient in the region. And although they are Muslim, I have never felt that the Hadendawa exert themselves unduly when it comes to such things as praying and fasting.

You are not exactly hit with education among the Hadendawa, for they cling to the old ways. Whether this is a result of government policy from Khartoum, a deliberate marginalization, or a Hadendawa pride in their own culture, I cannot say. Where other Sudanese are curious and welcoming, the Hadendawa come across as more insular in their dealings. But the Sudanese have a proverb for the situation: '*Adarawb waluf*.' This might be translated as 'The Hadendawa will not change their ways.' It's almost a case of 'Ignorance is bliss.'

In the *suq*, it being a Friday, things were slow in getting started, but a barber was already in action, grooming a man for a wedding. Apart from prayers, the three major weekend activities in Kassala seem to be drinking coffee, having a haircut and going to weddings. It wasn't really a good day for hanging around the *suq*, but one of the tailors was affable enough.

'If you are rich, this is the day when you lie in and have a nice, tasty pigeon for lunch, but people like me, we have to work Fridays to make ends meet.' He told me that his grandfather, or was it his great-grandfather, had been in the British army in the 1940s. He was Hausa, he said, and originally from Nigeria.

'We Africans are to be found anywhere in the world!' Throughout Sudan there are those whose ancestors from West Africa travelled here on the pilgrimage and, losing sight of either their goal or their home – for many would walk from West Africa – settled in Sudan.

Fighting against the British in this region of Sudan has been much more the norm than supporting them. One of the more entertaining clashes was between the Hadendawa and those intrepid explorers the Bakers. Returning to the land of the living after their discovery of Lake Albert as a secondary source of the Nile, the Bakers encountered skirmishing Hadendawa on their trek to Suakin. Nonplussed, Samuel Baker speared one Hadendawa warrior with his umbrella (even in the Sudan, an Englishman was not without his umbrella) while his wife-to-be Florence picked up a Hadendawa sword and put it to good use. After the mêlée Sam and Florrie felt in need of some refreshment, and 'broke up their lances to light a fire and boil coffee'.⁴ Sudan for the Bakers was at times a jaunt.

Kassala, however, should not be seen as a place solely Hadendawa; many of the merchant class are more typically 'Arab'. Near the barber's I found a narrow entrance, went down it and found myself in a coffee shop; by this I mean a yard with clay *zeers* of cool water and low stools to sit on. I salaamed on entering and the coffee maker returned my greeting.

'You're Egyptian, aren't you?'

'No, I'm not.'

'For sure you're Egyptian!'

'Well, I'm not.'

'Well, if you're not Egyptian, you could be part *khawaja* maybe, but only part.'

'Me? I tell you, I'm *khawaja pure*!'

Unusually for Sudan, however, there wasn't the usual warm invitation from the coffee drinkers to join them; this place had a somewhat different feel. The men present were very cleanly dressed with the

Beja tribesmen, Port Sudan

whitest of skull-caps, very shortly cropped hair and the pronounced beards that indicated a political outlook rather than, I guess, mere conservatism. They were all men of considerable stature. These, I think, were the local businessmen getting ready for Friday prayers. To do their ablutions they sat on *bambers*, the low wooden stools woven with rope, the ghastly plastic alternatives having not yet replaced the originals in Kassala. But even here there was an attempt at crossing bridges from their side.

security escort on the back of his motorbike to dip into breakfast together in a straw shelter in the *suq*.

This time, however, I was not heading out of town for camels, but was ostensibly in search of things sacred. Kassala is, perhaps, the spiritual heart of Sudan. Where the taxis waited I ignored the driver who approached me looking for a fare, walked past the one who looked a bit surly and opted for the one wearing the light, loose-fitting *arraqi* robe and *sirwal* trousers. I called out my destination.

'Khatmiyya!'

As we chatted the driver mistook me for a Syrian, for there are still residual hints of Damascus in my Arabic. He, too, had travelled and laughed as he remembered his wonderfully misspent youth in Dubai, working four days a week in the 'special forces' and making the most of the absence of *sharia* during the rest of the week.

'You can get everything in Dubai, everything!' I felt he wasn't talking about the shopping malls, and his wide grin reflected the good times. Finally convinced of my nationality, he told me more of life in Dubai, mentioning a people that I knew well.

'Those ones are mad for it!' I feigned disbelief.
'Really! And it's just them, is it?'
'It's the hot climate that does it, it's the climate!'

'You should take sugar in your coffee! It's good.'
'No, I'll get my sugar from natural fruit.' And indeed, the grapefruit of Kassala, grown in orchards that are watered with the seasonal flooding of the Gash river, have a lovely pink bloom on their skin and are second to none. But I was not going to spend the entire day indulging in coffee. It was time to get out of the town to the mountains.

When I had last come to Kassala, travel permission and photographic permission properly in order, I had set out at sunrise for a camel market beyond the town, beneath granite hills. But at the last moment there was a hitch; a young man at a checkpoint started to exercise his authority. In the end he suggested a compromise.

'You can take photographs of the camels, but not the men who are with them.'

'But that's ridiculous! What would the point of that be?' In the end he had followed on his motorbike, perhaps fearing an incident: 'westerner takes photograph of camel!' But I thought I knew what the issue was: we were just a few miles from the border with Eritrea and there is a secessionist movement in Kassala that is a response to the region's marginalization.

The tribesmen were affability itself, haggling and horse-playing together, and after the obligatory photographs of camels I ended up going off with the

Camel market, Kassala

untidily picnicked in the pillars' shade. The mosque itself was open to the sky, but the picnickers need not have worried about a passing shower. Legend has it that no matter how much the rain might lash down on Kassala, not a drop will fall on the mosque, such are the holy powers or *baraka* of the entombed sheikh. Just as the goodness of a person can bring a blessing to others while they are alive, so it is believed that a holy man's power to bless others does not end with his death. The reality, I suspect, is the impact of granite hills on precipitation. Another legend has it that just as the mosque was destroyed by an Uthman, in days to come an Uthman would restore it.

I can't imagine many of those picnicking had much of a sense of the history of Kassala's greatest monument and neither had I. I was told that the mosque had been destroyed by Mahdist forces but that seemed bizarre to me. Sudanese forces had swept into Ethiopia and burned the ancient churches of Gondor, destroying the wonderful ceilings where wide-eyed angels had gazed on congregations below. But why would they target a mosque?

Not every Islamic leader, however, had submitted to the Mahdi, although his forces were joined by Shilluk and Dinka as his movement became a national one. The spiritual leader of Kassala had opposed Mohammed Ahmed's claims to be the Mahdi and sided with the

My driver was not the only one from Kassala who had gone to Dubai. One of the Rashaida tribe had been taken there at a very young age to ride the camels in the races there; some of the Sudanese boys brought to Dubai are just eight or nine. But human rights groups objected to the use of children in this way; tied onto the camels, some would be seriously injured in racing accidents.

They now have robots instead of boys astride the camels in Dubai, no doubt an arrangement that is much better for the riders, who can now sit behind a desk in school. I suspect it is not just the races that are that bit duller. And by the age of 20, for the expiry date for boy jockeys is in their early-teens, the lad had returned to Kassala in search of his tribe.

The taxi dropped me near the mosque, with its wonderfully earthen brick dome at one end with the sticks that held it together protruding from the dome like unkempt hair. Here was buried the local holy man, al-Hassan, the son of the founder of the Khatmiyya order, one of the major Sufi orders in Sudan. It is perhaps the presence of the entombed al-Hassan and the Khatmiyya order that give the town of Kassala its spiritual atmosphere.

Religious buildings make wonderful ruins and the magnificent columns of the prayer hall hinted of imperial glory. This was the traditional Friday day out and families

Tomb of al-Hassan and the Khatmiyya Mosque, Kassala

The Italians were evicted from Kassala, presumably before their building-bridges project could be completed, and Anglo-Egyptian rule prevailed. How different Sudanese cuisine might be today if, instead of the British, the Italians had held sway a little longer!

Near the mosque, under a spreading acacia tree, were the usual stalls selling knick-knacks, framed portraits of past sheikhs, male and female, prayer beads and head-cloths. I didn't want a plastic set of rosaries as a souvenir, for the traditional prayer beads of dried seeds can be quite lovely.

'Have you got anything here that isn't made in China?' The stall keeper finally came up with a string of wooden rosary beads.

'And what kind of wood are they made of? Is it *nebak*?' This is the wild thorn tree that bears little apple-like fruit. The stall-keeper had the answer on the tip of his tongue.

'I know, but I've forgotten the word. You get a kind of oil from it. Now I've got it; it's *zeitoun*!'

'*Zeitoun*! But olives don't grow in Sudan, do they? My God, you guys, even the material for your prayer beads is imported!'

I left for the tomb of another celebrated holy man, just a few minutes' walk away. Sheikhs' tombs are the landmarks of the Sudanese landscape and this one did

status quo, the Turko-Egyptian authorities. Mahdist forces had in turn defeated the Khatmiyya order who opposed them, with Uthman Digna destroying both the mosque and the tomb.

Just as the main political parties in Ireland today still reflect the divisions of the civil war, so two of the main parties in the North of Sudan still reflect the divisions of over a century ago when the followers of the Mahdi, the *Ansar*, and the Khatmiyya order of Kassala were enemies. The former Prime Minister Sadiq al-Mahdi inherits not only the Mahdi's spiritual credentials but is head of the Umma Party. Similarly, the head of the Khatmiyya Sufi order is head of the Democratic Unionist Party. For at least two parties, political power is essentially a family matter: the son inherits from the father his position as spiritual leader and leader of the party.

A more extraordinary version of the history of the mosque was that Kassala's greatest monument was re-built by Italians. Italian forces had occupied the area on at least two occasions: when fighting the Mahdi's forces and later in the 1940s. I found their apparent mosque-building a bit hard to believe however; why would the Italians want to build a mosque next to a tomb in Kassala? Was it a wish to curry favour with the locals, just as Napoleon, on his conquest of Egypt, had presented the French Revolution as embracing ideas central to Islam?

not disappoint. Such places delight with their coolness and mats were spread out under the trees. A labourer and a man I took to be the gaffer welcomed me with the usual Sudanese affability. Ahmed laboured in the orchards of Kassala that gave the town its epithet *Kassala al-khadra*, Kassala the Green.

'*Ta'ban!*' he said. 'I'm so tired!'

'Yes, it must be hard work!' I wondered what exactly he meant, for in Sudanese Arabic the word *ta'ban* has multiple meanings.

'And are you married?' I asked.

'I'm still single. *Ta'ban!*' The head of the group joined us, wonderfully proud, along with a mechanic, just a little fat from good living, who like many a Sudanese wanted to tell me about Ireland.

'How come you still have the British ruling part of your country?' He went on to explain our political situation to the others.

'They have so many problems in Ireland!'

Given the millions dead from the 'jihad' against the South, the millions displaced from the current conflict in Darfur and the likely break away of the South as an independent country, this did seem to me at the time a little rich. The Sudanese do love to talk about Ireland, however, usually referring to that famous film of Irish rebellion, *Braveheart*.

I had had a similar experience in one of the chicken restaurants in the market town of Gedaref a few days earlier. The restaurant walls were covered in the same kind of roll-on murals depicting the stately home with the lawns and begonia beds that grace restaurant walls in Yemen, overlooking the men coming in for their chicken fresh from the spit. One of the waiters engaged in conversation as the *shawarma* on the spit dripped fat.

'And where are you from?'

'Ireland.'

'Which Ireland?'

'I only know of one.'

'There are two.'

'Really? And Sudan, how many Sudans are there, tell me?'

'One!'

'Well, Ireland is just like Sudan then, isn't it?'

Here at the sheikh's tomb, political matters, rather than things spiritual, seemed to reign and we moved on to talk about the Chinese. The relationship between Sudan and the Chinese is a strange one. Jilted by both the US and the UK, I suppose Sudan has fallen into the arms of the Chinese, but I suspect quite a few Sudanese still prefer the old flames. I had seen this scepticism towards the Chinese 'friendship' with Sudan when I was passing by Friendship Hall in Khartoum late one

Tomb, Kassala

afternoon as a warm official welcome was being given to Chinese dignitaries. Outside in Nile Avenue, a Tuti Islander greeted me wryly.

'Have you seen the celebrations?'

'Joyful indeed! It's just like a wedding!'

'It's the Chinese and the National Congress together!' And it was quite a celebration, with musicians blowing on long horns, like those they have in Blue Nile State, that were the height of the men themselves, and women trilling ecstatically.

'But isn't it strange that the Islamists should be so close to the communists?'

'Here they call the communists *kuffar* if they are Sudanese. But if they are foreign they welcome them!' That was in Khartoum. Here in Kassala, however, my companions extolled Chinese virtues.

'How hard-working they are!'

'You never see a fat Chinese!'

'Look at all the great things they are doing for the Sudan!'

'They don't even need a fridge or even a *zeer* to cool their water, but drink straight from the tap!'

As I left, the sheikh offered me water from the *zeer*. In my youth I might have accepted, but now, as even the middle-class Sudanese are pampered with bottled mineral water, I tactlessly refused the proffered cup.

Zeers

But I think I know why the Chinese, like me, might choose not to drink from the lovely clay *zeers*, slightly algaed over beneath the shade of a cooling neem tree: all and sundry drink from the *zeer*, or rather from the cup or tin can left by it, and as a result the amoebic content of the water can be incredibly rich.

It's a tradition to drink from the holy spring on the lower slopes of Toteel Mountain and, like drinking from the Nile, they say that if you drink once you will be sure to return. But the Friday crowds were gathering and with the *shebab* and the *chicks* heading towards the cafés on the lower slopes for an afternoon of innocent flirtation, this was not my idea of enjoyment.

Back at the main mosque, worshippers were doing their ablutions before sunset. Some of the lads at the Quranic school called me over and offered to put me up in their institution. That was the young; not far from the mosque there were the rooms where the elderly stayed; it seemed that I had come across the Sudanese version of an old people's home.

I took a minibus back to Kassala. But as we approached the town, I thought I saw a Nuban celebration with a horned dancer in the midst. But this was not Kordofan but Kassala, and the gathering was surely not a Nuban wrestling contest. I desperately clicked my fingers at the conductor, jumped off the bus and paid my fare.

It was, of course, the Sufis who were gathering outside the mosque and these inheritors of Khatmiyya traditions were having a good time as the sun dipped towards the horizon. The sheikh was not a Nuban wearing the horns of a bull above his headdress, but a young man wearing a Lord Nelson-shaped hat of many colours. The drummers banged their drums as the worshippers moved in a circle, the darkest in complexion of the group expressing his joy in a somersault or two. This was more upbeat than anything I had come across in Khartoum and was as joyful and welcoming a religious gathering as others, to the outsider at least, are dour. As soon as the sun set it all stopped and I approached the young sheikh, giving a mimed kiss of his hand. He must have sensed my thoughts.

'Not everyone approves of what we do!' I told him which expression of Islam appealed to me.

In the morning, I left before sunrise. The morning star hung above the town and, as I walked through the narrow streets of the *suq*, it seemed as if 100 competing muezzins, each echoing the call of the other, were sounding out in the half-light. It reminded me of my time in Sana'a, perhaps the most beautiful city in the Arab world, founded by a son of Noah they say, its mosques and tiered homes still marvellously intact within the city walls, each dawn alive with a thousand competing calls to prayer issuing from the minarets and ushering in the daylight. Apart from the Sufis, the dawn call to prayer seemed the most energetic thing I encountered in that lovely, languid town, whose inhabitants, I am told, still await the coming of an Uthman who will restore their mosque to its former glory.

NOTES

1 Junker, Wilhelm, *Travels in Africa During the Years 1875–1886* (London: Chapman and Hall, 1890) p.107
2 Ibid. p.102
3 Ibid. p.111
4 Thompson, op. cit. p.107

CHAPTER SIX

THE CORAL CITY OF SUAKIN

The journey from Kassala had been a long one, and passing through those landscapes of sand stretching to hills of black stone, graced occasionally with a branching acacia and a few Beja huts of woven mats covering frames, the hereafter that Islam promised could not have contrasted more with the realities of life in Sudan.

Suakin, too, was a world apart from the one through which I was travelling. Five centuries ago, a Portuguese captain had surveyed from his ship an island almost perfectly round in a circular nook. The island was a self-contained city, a world within itself, where every square foot was built on, 'so that all the island is a city, and all the city an island'.[1] The island defined the city and the city crowned the island. Suakin was an intact world, one mile square, that cast a network over the seas, with ships sailing to Egypt and India and Abyssinia. It was one of a few Red Sea ports with

traditional Islamic architecture, like Jeddah and the ports of the Yemeni coast.

'Jeddah? There's a boat leaving today. Jeddah?'

As far as harassing a traveller goes, the guys hanging out where the bus stopped were about as benign as drivers touting for custom can get. But I wasn't Saudi-bound, although a ferry still leaves Suakin regularly. I had reached my destination: the coral city of Suakin, with its merchant houses and mosques 'built from the deep' from madropore, rock coral.

Suakin was a place that dreams were made of. It was architecturally the perfect Islamic city, largely built of indigenous materials according to the traditions of the ports of the Red Sea. The merchant homes were graced with trellised bay windows called *mashrabiyas*, from which the women of the house viewed the street as if through a veil, the window trellis casting patterns of light and shadow within the room.

The architect Jean-Pierre Greenlaw, seeing Suakin as a fading miracle of Islam, documented the coral buildings that still survived in the 1950s in his exquisite book, *The Coral Buildings of Suakin*. It wasn't just that the spiral staircases carried the sea breezes throughout the merchants' homes, or that the doors were of Java teak, or that the motifs carved into wood would have been mirrored in the patterns of the women's dresses. For Greenlaw, the whole city expressed a common, uniting ethos: Islam.

I gently mocked the owner of the maroon Mazda that would take me into town.

'I'd say this thing is from the time of the Mahdi himself!' The driver was as decent as they come, driving around until we found a hotel that would accept a foreigner travelling with Sudanese-issued ID, not a passport. The hotel reception area was decorated with a stencil design to imitate wallpaper. Its residents would be mostly Sudanese travelling to Saudi Arabia for work and, at the right time of year, the *hajj*. Suakin had been a major port for Sudanese and West Africans going on pilgrimage, with a nearby island serving as a quarantine station.

'Can I have a room upstairs?'

'Upstairs it's the roof, but you can sleep there if you want!'

My first stop was the city gates, built by Kitchener as the British tried to assert their control on this rebellious part of Sudan in their desire to avenge Gordon's ignominious defeat. The city wall Kitchener had built around Suakin had disappeared, but the city gate, with the hand against the Evil Eye still painted by the door, stood pretty much intact. Although the monument had featured on the old Sudanese ten pound note, it was not exactly protected with loving care: a load of pipes had been dumped on the far side and one of the twin cannon had disappeared under the invading scrub. The monument smelt as if it now functioned as the public lavatory. A policeman rushed over.

'You're not allowed to take photographs!'

'Why not?'

'You need to get permission from the authorities in town!' I waved my permit in his face.

Wandering into town, I found closed-up shops and a rather miserable market. There was something distinctive about one of the passers-by, however, and I stopped to greet him.

'But are you Sudanese?'

'No, I'm Yemeni. We've just come by boat.'

'And how long did it take?'

'Two days from Mukallah to Aden then two days from Aden to here.'

The Shata Gate

Burckhardt writes that a significant number of the Suakin merchants in his day were from Hadramaut in Yemen,[2] and the Suakin merchants liked to buy Dongola horses at Shendi to export to the Yemen.[3] Indeed, Suakin has its twin town across the Red Sea in the port of Al Luhaiyah on the coast of the Tihamah plain.

I had once pitched my tent there in the abandoned port, savouring the *diwans* of the crumbling Turkish houses and the bay silted over with mangrove swamps. Further along the coast in Hodeidah I had chatted with the labourers in the tobacco *suq* where the Turkish mansions were crumbling one by one, a sledgehammer inducing their final collapse. Apart from the bats that were the only occupants of the Turkish houses, Al Luhaiyah had been pretty much deserted. Nor was Suakin exactly buzzing. In 1876, when Junker arrived in Suakin from Egypt, he walked down a thoroughfare of lively crowds and side streets ringing with the sounds of armourers, smiths and leather craftsmen. In those days, an entire street was given over to barbers, for the Beja tribesmen have high-maintenance hairdos with hair stacked high above the head and topped with a deftly-set wooden comb. The hair oil used to keep the whole pack of cards in place was from the butcher's, the mutton fat 'taken fresh from the shambles' and chewed into a workable paste before it was rubbed into the hair.[4]

On the day of my visit there wasn't a barber in sight, and I wondered what the contemporary town would have to offer. In the past, trains of 1,000 camels had left for the interior and Sudan's Arabic gum and ivory were exported from Suakin. But today I found nothing more out of the ordinary than turtle shells for sale, an unfortunate ending for such a wonderful marine animal. And that was about as exotic as contemporary Suakin got.

At least the coffee would be good, I thought, with Ethiopia as a distant neighbour. However, I watched in dismay as the café patron dispatched a swarm of flies that resettled on the *finjans* and sugar.

'And are you going to the island?' I was a bit confused.

'Island?'

'Old Suakin, of course!'

In 1885, the British officer Gambier Parry, posted to Sudan to fight Mahdist forces, describes the nature of the city. There was the town proper, with 'low, flat-topped houses of the ordinary Eastern type',[5] joined by a causeway to a suburb on the mainland with mosques that had outgrown the town. Finally, there was the 'native town' of huts made of grass matting.

I still had to cross over to Suakin proper. In the past, ferries carried the wealthy back and forth to the island, the less well-off simply wading across, until General Gordon had the causeway built to the island town, a scene now picturesque with a rainbowed line of fishing boats.

I entered the island town through a reconstruction of the gates that Gordon had built, with their two oval spaces in the walls that had once allowed guns to be fired from the shelter of the gates. Two mortars still marked the entrance to the ancient town, and the spot by the walls that had once housed Egyptian troops now accommodated a few policemen.

Suakin was a city defined not just by the sea but by Islam. For Greenlaw, Islamic and nomadic traditions were reflected in the sparse furnishings of the merchant homes; although settled, the merchants were still travelling light. The floors would have been simply graced with mats and even the wealthy would have eaten from the communal dish placed on the floor. The inhabitants would have slept on the roof, enjoying the night breeze beneath the stars in the traditional bed of wood and woven strips of hide, the *angarib*, nicely described by Burckhardt as 'a bed for the night, and a sofa in the day'.[6]

I wondered, however, about the Islamic 'unity' of Suakin. Suakin, surely, must always have been an almost schizophrenic place, with a cosmopolitan Arab trading class living in their exquisite houses on the island, while the indigenous Beja slummed it on the outskirts of the

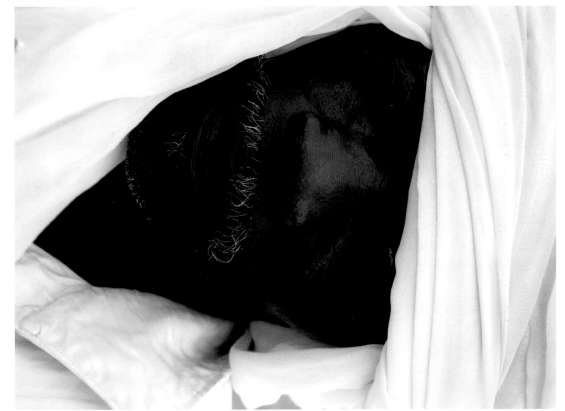

Suakin fisherman

mainland town. And although the Beja are Muslim, they do not come across as much versed in Islam.

In the mainland town, the indigenous language of the Beja would have dominated. Parry listed the Babel of languages that confronted him in Suakin, ranging from Portuguese to Armenian to Punjabi and Hindustani. A similar wealth of languages can be seen today on the headstones in the British graveyard in Khartoum, the best-maintained green area in the city.

The buildings of Suakin are not only Turkish; Egyptian architecture followed in the later nineteenth century. The legendary caravanserai on the mainland, once rumoured to have 365 rooms, was built when Suakin seemed set to enjoy boom years that never materialized. As I walked around the island I found one of the major Egyptian monuments, the Customs Building, was not quite as imposing as it used to be; once topped by a lion, its entrance gate was now lion-less and propped up by wooden supports.

After this was the *Muhafaza*, with its fine gateway flanked by cannon, but I would be venturing up neither of the ramps of steps: everything was in a state of collapse. As when a coastal settlement is swept by a tsunami, with just a few solitary buildings rising above the general destruction, so the city I viewed that day was just a few sad remnants rising above the rubble.

Was Suakin ever anything but a rundown place? It was hard to imagine it as a centre of international commerce. Even when Burckhardt had passed through in 1814, of the 600 houses of Suakin proper he wrote that two-thirds were in ruins, 'for the madrepore with which they are built soon decays, unless constantly kept in repair'.[7] Burckhardt just managed to leave Suakin alive. He was accused of being a spy for the Mamlukes. In response, the explorer (he usually travelled in disguise as Sheikh Ibrahim Abdullah) produced the *firmaans* he had concealed on his person and that guaranteed him protection, one with the seal of Mohammed Ali, the other with the seal of Ibrahim Pasha, his son. The *Bey* immediately changed his tune and Burckhardt had a free place on the sailing boat to Jeddah.

The whole island city of Suakin had been fatally flawed. As long as the outer layer of lime plaster was maintained, the Turkish merchant houses could survive centuries. Once that protective layer was no longer renewed, the humid salt air ate away the very fabric of the buildings. As the old city decayed, to the utter indifference of the authorities, streets were declared unsafe, conservationists dithered and the merchant houses were ransacked for materials to build the shanty town.

As I stood near the *Muhafaza* I was not entirely alone. A Sudanese from Jebel Aulia, a dam on the White Nile

Customs Gateway

The *Muhafaza*

with strong military traditions, attempted to teach the visitor a bit of history.

'This was the house of Uthman Digna!'

Suakin is linked to the fortunes of the Mahdi's lieutenant, who had not only destroyed Kassala's most famous mosque but had also taken on British-Egyptian forces. The troops of Uthman Digna were equipped with spears and swords and shields of crocodile skin. In contrast, according to the officer Parry, the British army were a select force, armed with the latest equipment but unable to see the point of their being in Sudan – a situation comparable perhaps to that of western forces in the Islamic world today.

Armed with spears and shields against infantry with Martini rifles, Uthman Digna's men slaughtered an Anglo-Egyptian force not far from Suakin. They later did what no enemy of the British Empire had done before: the Beja broke through the key British defence arrangement, the 'square', and caused havoc within.

The arch-imperialist Rudyard Kipling celebrated the courage of the Hadendawa, called Fuzzy Wuzzies by the British, in the dialect of a soldier:

We've fought with many men acrost the seas,
An' some of 'em was brave an' some was not:
The Paythan an' the Zulu an' Burmese;
But the Fuzzy was the finest o' the lot.[8]

Commemoration stone, the *Muhafaza*

They also left their mark on a soldier who survived his time under Kitchener to enjoy the age of television: Lance Corporal Jones in the BBC series *Dad's Army*.

Throughout the empire, no one had fought with a bravery to match Sudan's Beja. But had Uthman Digna built the monument now collapsing before me? Even as they lost much of the Sudan, British-Egyptian forces had held on to Suakin. Western and Sudanese versions of history often seem to follow parallel lines that just cannot meet. Where the Sudanese saw the building before me as the abode of their national

even then the mosque nearby was open to the stars. I walked through its arches to find a pulpit still delicately carved and reminiscent of the towns of Tihamah across the way in Yemen. There, the main port of al-Luhaiyah had silted up and been abandoned, the intricate plaster of its *diwans* crumbling in the humid, salty air. The traditions of the *sambuks*, the gorgeously-painted dhows of the Tihamah coast, however, survive and they still plough the Red Sea.

The fate of Suakin has not been much different from its neighbour across the Red Sea. For a place of such romance – apart from the inconvenient truth of its dependence on slavery – Suakin's final demise was brought about by something quite mundane: the British wanted a port to accommodate their steamers, but the entrance through Suakin waters was too tricky. Port Sudan was built instead. The merchants relocated down the road and their houses were stripped to build the shacks of those further down the social ladder, Beja rather than Turkish or Egyptian. The delicate latticing that had graced some merchant's home, perhaps now formed part of a hut. As for the desolation around me, no one apart from the occasional lover of architecture much cared about the loss.

The textures of Suakin are today not so much teak and coral as rusted corrugated iron, walls of oil drums,

hero, I could picture Gordon or Kitchener enjoying, if not a whisky on the terrace, at least the sea view. I voiced my doubts.

'I don't think Uthman Digna built this place.' Above the main gate there was a crescent, an emblem I assumed of Turko-Egyptian rule, but such confrontations rarely lead anywhere.[9] It goes far beyond issues such as who built a residence. Some even claim that Suakin's buildings had been restored by the Mahdi in 1881– a surprising role for the Guided One.[10]

Talking with trainees in class, it's clear that to Muslim Sudanese Uthman Digna is a national hero who fought occupation. What has been conveniently airbrushed out of the picture is that he was a slave trader; he may have liberated Sudan from Turko-Egyptian rule but he also sold his fellow Sudanese as a commodity. It will be denied of course, but the major commodity exported from Suakin was the Sudanese themselves: African Sudanese would have left Suakin either as pilgrims or slaves. Burckhardt writes that since the slavers would sometimes disguise slaves as pilgrims in order to avoid the tax on slaves, so pilgrims came to be taxed too.[11]

In today's Suakin, there were few homes left to contemplate. Apart from Uthman Digna's/Kitchener's place, there was hardly even the shell of a merchant house left standing. A couple of mosques survived, but

fences of cooking oil tins and sea-washed wood, a not unpleasing aesthetic. The shanty town has its own vibrant life. When I was invited into one of the shacks my host played the traditional stringed instrument, the *oud*, for me as light sifted into the room through the walls of knotted planks.

As I retreated that day from the general desolation of Suakin to the mainland town, I caught sight of a couple of camels grazing, a reminder of the camel trains that had once left Suakin for the interior. At the end of the causeway was a restaurant shack of cobalt blue promising fish. The proprietor however looked amazed at my request.

'Fish!'

'Yes, fish! The sea is just a few yards away, isn't it?'

'Yes, but the time of day!' It was almost sunset and eating fish at such a time was apparently out of the question. The fish-eater in Suakin will not eat alone: the local cats are famous for their bad table manners and demand that diners share their seafood with them. Sitting under a tree once in Khartoum, as I drank my tea a Sudanese told me of his dining experience when he had visited the Red Sea coast. As he was eating, he had felt something touch his leg and, looking down, encountered a cat holding out its paw, begging for fish. Startled, he leapt up and asked the waiter if the

restaurant was inhabited by *jinn*. The Sudanese do speak of Suakin as a place *miskuun* or haunted, and one popular etymology of the word 'Suakin' links it to *sawajin* (prisons) for according to legend the prophet Suleiman imprisoned *jinn* on Suakin.

Despite the preponderance of cats and *jinn*, I was able to enjoy a chat with the proprietor's son, who was studying statistics in the University of Port Sudan. With a Yemeni father and a Sudanese mother, he wore the sarong of the Yemeni coast beneath his Sudanese *arraqi*. He had already married at 20, his wife too being Sudanese-Yemeni. He had an enquiring mind. Unlike the Sudanese who usually ask the traveller what dishes he has eaten and laugh at whether he has tried *umm-fitt-fitt* (a hangover cure of raw meat, lemon and chilli) or *comboneea* (stinking sheep's intestine), he wanted to see things from the traveller's perspective.

'What is it that most annoys you when you are travelling in Sudan?'

I had quite a list. There was the need for travel permission; being taken from the bus at checkpoints; the need to report to 'Security' before checking into a hotel. But there was also, even when the foreigner has a reasonable command of Arabic, the Sudanese equivalent of 'Does he take sugar?' It is not just when travelling that the *khawaja* can be dealt with as a non-

The Yemeni influence

person. Arriving with my counterpart at a new project one day, I was ignored by the secretary, who turned to the Sudanese with me and asked, 'Does he pray?' My counterpart, who scarcely knew me from Adam, announced that I didn't, for in his way of reckoning I wasn't a Muslim and, therefore, couldn't in any proper sense be said to pray.

My Sudanese-Yemeni host continued his gentle questioning.

'And what is it that most delights you when you travel?' I could have enumerated the joys of travel among the Sudanese: their spontaneity; their genial welcoming of a stranger; their incredible good humour; their sharing of provisions on the road; the way they let you into their circle as they sip tea together. Instead, I just looked him in the eye, for that mixing of Yemeni and Sudanese genes had produced rather attractive results, and laughed.

He later pointed out his house near the lovely Taj al Sir Mosque with its extensive wooden pulpit above the central courtyard.

'And do you both still live with your father?'

'Oh no! My father has married five times.' That was one more than the allowance, but presumably divorce had preceded the marriage to the fifth, or perhaps he was gently mocking the foreigner.

Taj al Sir Mosque, mainland Suakin

Now in the evening, the mainland town had gained some life. A lad from Khartoum asked if I wanted *Zamzam* water from the sacred spring. Women from Eritrea or Ethiopia served coffee with frankincense burning in clay censers, holding court before the migrants back from Saudi Arabia. After their time abroad, they must have enjoyed the chance to flirt again. A boat had just come in, and now I was the one asking the questions.

'And how long were you there?'

'Thirteen years.'

archetypal figures too: the seafarer, the pilgrim, the boy with the camel at the well. In that almost desolate landscape, lightened only by the warm glow of the lamps where the women make tea, I watched one old, blind man being led by another old man, joined together by a stick. It could have been a scene from a play by Samuel Beckett.

Port Sudan, the upstart port that had brought about Suakin's ruin, beckoned.

'They have a new promenade there. You must see it!' I wasn't sure that walking among crowds would be much my scene.

'And Zain are having an exhibition!' A display by a mobile phone company settled the matter. Port Sudan could wait.

I turned out to be wrong in my prejudice. Port Sudan is in fact a lovely, languid place, at least in winter. With its wide sweep of clean streets and paved ways, and with the Beja reclining on the promenade over coffee and cards, and the lads playing billiards in the open air as a ship unloads at the docks, it has a good blend of the colonial, the modern, and the tribal.

That night I slept through the cold winter winds on the hotel roof, but there was a full moon and when the electricity went off I woke to Orion the Hunter brilliant in the desert sky.

'And how often did you get home?'

'Never!'

I don't know what the returnee had to show for his time abroad, hopefully more than just the mobile phone the likes of which I had never seen before. He was ecstatic at being back in Sudan. And he spoke of things you would not hear on the news. Back on home ground, he laughed at the Saudis with contempt. He would never go to Saudi Arabia again he swore and, with a voice that I felt was perhaps too loud, spoke of his plans. He would go to Europe next time.

'Those Saudis they love the Americans. They would kiss their hands!' Hands? I thought his language here showed considerable restraint.

It seemed that I had reached the far margins of Sudan where life was more interesting than at the heart of some homogenous group. But Suakin had its

View from Taj al Sir Mosque door, Suakin

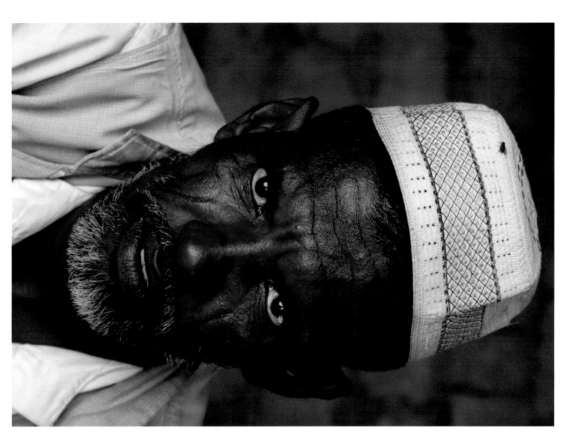

Beja portrait, mainland Suakin

Ruins, Suakin mainland

On the promenade, Port Sudan

CHAPTER SIX: THE CORAL CITY OF SUAKIN

159

I had arrived in Suakin decades too late, for like a dream, the legendary city had disappeared. Junker had described Suakin 'as a very daughter of the sea, its merchant houses themselves a product of the deep'.[12] It now seemed that the sea had reclaimed what it had given. Its soul, however, survives in *The Coral Buildings of Suakin*. Greenlaw's book includes the pencil drawings of Shennawi's house number 163, with its ground-floor shops and the *diwan* framed by its pointed arch. On another page is the house of Omar Effendi Obeid, 'imposing rather than intimate'. And here is Khorshid Effendi's house, with the walls of the *diwan*, he writes, 'covered with geometric and floral arabesques',[13] now revealed for all to see since the collapse of the front wall of the house. Later pages have the details: the panelling designs that graced a bay window; the fretted wooden lunettes; the lattice work grilles through which the light that had danced on the sea sifted into the women's quarters, the woodwork itself 'almost playful with its fret-work exuberance'.[14]

Like a city bombed from the air, only a few isolated monuments have survived. All that now remains of Suakin is a labour of love written by a foreign architect living in Sudan and the memories, perhaps, of some

merchant families now inhabiting villas in Port Sudan. The 'daughter of the sea', like a spirit, has melted into air, thin air. Nothing remains but a heap of rubble. But the other Suakin, the antithesis of the merchant city, still has a thriving exuberance.

NOTES

1 Greenlaw, Jean-Pierre, *The Coral Buildings of Suakin: Islamic Architecture, Planning, Design and Domestic Arrangements in a Red Sea Port* (Keegan Paul International, 1995) p.9

2 Burckhardt, op. cit. p.48

3 Ibid. p.321

4 Junker, op. cit. p.56

5 Parry, Gambier, *Suakin, 1885: Being a Sketch of the Campaign of This Year*, (London: Kegan Paul, Trench and Co., 1886) p.23

6 Burckhardt, op. cit. p.213

7 Burckhardt, op. cit. p.432

8 Kipling, Rudyard, *Barrack-Room Ballads* (NuVision Publications, 2008) p.11

9 Greenlaw writes that the Muhafazah was built by Mumtaz Pasha in 1866. Greenlaw, op. cit. p.73

10 www.sudan.net/

11 Burckhardt, op. cit. p.462

12 Junker, op. cit. p.51

13 Greenlaw, op. cit. p.26

14 Ibid. p.58

CHAPTER SEVEN

IN THE LAND OF KUSH

On New Year's Day I couldn't get a boat across the Nile. I had travelled 5 hours north of Khartoum to Karima, a nondescript town that is surrounded by some of Sudan's most picturesque villages. It being a public holiday, the *suq* was dead quiet, and there wasn't a lot of life on the river. Dumped on the banks lay the old steamers that once linked the settlements by the Nile with the train system at Karima. With the development of the road system and the new bridge built by the Chinese – 'Friendship Bridge' of course – the pontoons that used to ferry people, livestock and cars across the Nile were mostly idle. Even the train station has fallen into disuse and vendors spread their wares on the tracks.

I had travelled one starry night on a boat – one of those low flat boats with a sail and a prominent rudder that are sometimes found in this part of Sudan – along with two brothers carrying palm leaves from Kerma

to Karima, but now, apart from the rowing boats acting as ferries, or the boats taking the islanders near Dongola to town, there was scarcely a boat on the river.

There was hardly a soul in the *suq*. Taking advantage of the holiday and because of the cold weather people were sleeping late. At night I had gone to bed with two jumpers on, but I knew it would be intensely hot by midday. Now, in the early-morning light, a few policemen huddling around a tea woman invited me to join them and I enjoyed their banter. I caught one of them later in his thick winter coat; having finished his shift he was now moonlighting as a rickshaw driver.

In the *suq* I started to negotiate the fare over to Nuri on the other bank. Nuri to me was the archetypal Sudanese village by the Nile: men riding donkeys along dirt tracks that sent up a cloud of golden dust; light sifting through palm trees on to villagers chatting beneath; men weeding the fields by the river to the chugging sound of the irrigation pumps and maybe stopping to smoke a joint as the sun set above the far bank.

'How much is it to Nuri?'

'How much are you offering?'

'The appropriate fare.'

'Then offer it. How much?'

'You say!' And so it went on, until Abdu finally offered to take me for 20 Sudanese pounds. We agreed on 15.

We drove past Jebbel Berkel. From the mountain top the previous evening I had seen the sun set beyond the pyramids on the last day of the year, and I had earlier joined the Sudanese exploring the ruins beneath the mountain, for this had been the religious centre of the Kushite kingdom of Napata. As the red band of light faded on the horizon, with the plain stretching to the blue ribbon of the Nile and beyond, the lines in the sand appeared like ripples on a beach, and the group of royal pyramids, collapsing over the centuries into rubble in the sand, hinted of former kingdoms.

Two centuries before my trip to Karima, a fellow of Trinity College Cambridge, George Waddington, had left Cairo in 1820 on 'an antiquarian visit', entering the Sudan with camels, mules, guides and a dog,

Abandoned steamers

Taking the milk from the island by ferry, Dongola

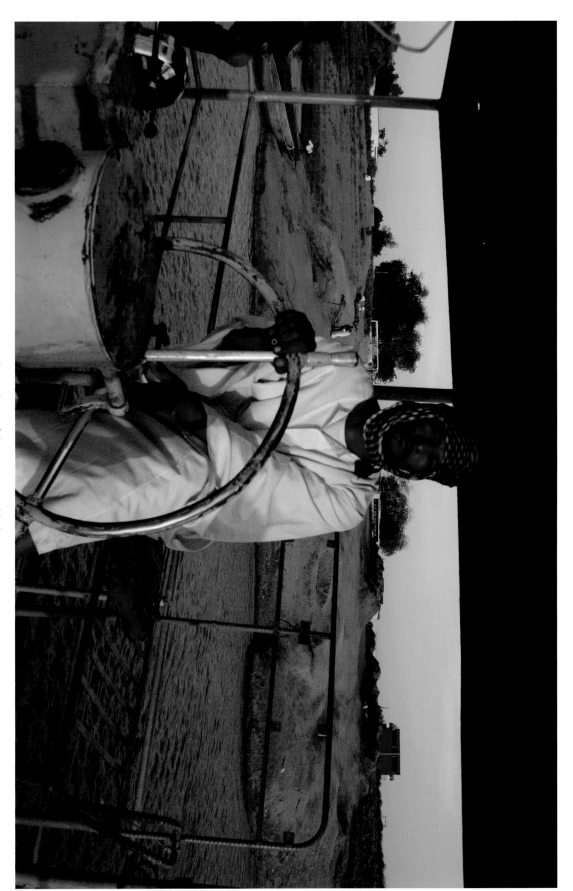

Last days of the pontoon, Karima

Temple at Jebbel Berkel

Anubis.[1] Arriving near Jebbel Berkel after dark, it had at first seemed that temple columns rose the height of the sandstone table mountain. In the light of day, however, Waddington could see that the 'column' was not man-made. He sensitively described Jebbel Berkel in his journal as having 'an irregularity in its outline' which fixed the traveller's gaze;[2] in fact the mountain culminates in a monumental phallus. This must have been what originally attracted worshippers to the site; it may later have become the centre for the worship of Ammun, the god believed to bring fecundity to Egypt with the Nile floods, but there must once have been a more explicit celebration of fertility.

Waddington did not get the chance to travel further south, as the authorities denied him travel permission – a situation not unfamiliar to those travelling in Sudan today. Exploring the ruins at Jebbel Berkel and Merowe, he asked a key question: had Egypt determined the nature of worship in this part of Africa, or vice versa? He decides in favour of African origins, saying that the Egyptian divinities, temples and tombs had their genesis in Ethiopia, a term then used to cover much of Sudan. His conclusion that the culture originated in Africa would not be unpopular in some circles today.

As the Egyptians extended their power over this part of Sudan, they had seen not just a phallus in Jebbel Berkel but a serpent crowned with a sun disk symbolizing kingship. With their primary god Ammun so explicit in the landscape itself, the Egyptians claimed a god-given right to rule this part of Sudan.

In the *laconda* in the *suq*, where a bed in a room with three others cost just a few Sudanese pounds, one of the Egyptian labourers had expressed a not dissimilar view. Egypt's burgeoning population was still spilling into Sudan, and the labourer seemed not to give any offence to his Sudanese companion when he said, '*Al balad wahid*. It's all one country!' He wasn't referring to Sudan as one country, but to Sudan and Egypt as one.

For some Sudanese there might have been something poignant about this year's New Year celebrations. New Year's Day was the official day for celebrating independence from the British, at least in the North; they are not so enthusiastic in Juba about what Sudan's independence brought. But this was probably going to be the last year in which Sudan would officially be one country, although few were saying such a thing aloud.

Within ten days the Southern Sudanese would be voting as to whether or not to have their own separate state of South Sudan. It looked likely that the referendum would formally bring about a separate state. A proposed national anthem had now been written, but what would the new country be called?

Egyptian guest in the *laconda*

A lot of people were going for Kush. Kush? The land in which I was now travelling had once been known as Kush, with the Kingdom of Napata here at Jebbel Berkel and the Kingdom of Meroe, once written about by the Greek historian Herodotus, further south. Why on earth would the Southern Sudanese want to see their country as a latter day Kush?

Life here in Karima, however, was far from either capital. As we drove along the palm-fringed road, Abdu turned to me.

'Do you know, they say in Khartoum that we are backward?'

'And why's that?'

'Because we live in houses like these. When the electricity goes off we just sit in the yard in the shade of the trees.'

The homes of Karima seemed rather idyllic to me, with their yards, bright metal gates and flat roofs beneath sheltering palms. Their *jalous* walls made the indigenous architecture much cooler in summer than a tin-roofed restaurant or a flat in Khartoum Two. On one rocky outcrop a circular pigeon house rose above the homes.

'And the palms? When do you harvest the dates?'

'Around October. These plantations here are new. Before this it was just empty land.'

'Well, it's good to see something has developed!'

Guest in the *laconda*

As we drove, a Karima singer sounded out from the cassette, accompanied by the tight rhythms of the traditional *tambour*, a banjo-like instrument.

'I love that music!'

'This?'

'Yes, I can't stand the stuff on the electric organ.'

'We used to make the *tambour* from the gourd.' I had only ever seen it made from either an empty tin, such as those used for a litre or more of vegetable oil, but I loved its wild, tight sounds.

Whether you were in the capital or a neglected village, it seemed that there were few interruptions to life's rhythms. There were the natural rhythms of the year, when the Nile rose and enriched the islands if it flooded. Social life was visiting your relatives, the routine broken occasionally by a wedding when you saw your relatives again.

The night before, there had been nothing in Karima to hint of New Year apart from a group of *shebab* sharing a bowl of jelly in the restaurant. In Khartoum, they drive around in the early hours of the morning, the city becoming one big traffic jam. However, given all those date plantations, I'm sure that behind closed doors some of the lads would have been knocking back the *araquay*.

It was now mid-winter, peak tourist season in Sudan, and there were maybe half a dozen intrepid travellers staying in the *lacondas* of the town. I had celebrated New Year's Eve with a Brazilian traveller and a plastic bottle of Fanta. The Brazilian, new to Sudan, had been fascinated by Islam.

'Those lines of men getting ready to pray! It's their faith that interests me!'

After my years in Sudan, I was a little more cynical. The religious situation in the Arabic-speaking world cannot be very different from how it was in Britain in Victorian days, or in Ireland until very recently: there was the public conformity to religion – not going to public worship might have had repercussions on your chances of employment for example – with public piety perhaps matched by less public expressions of the self, especially when abroad.

'Faith is one word for it. Conforming to something in public is another possibility. I mean, what happens if you don't pray?' Pleasure seeking in Brazil was a more public affair.

'It will never happen in Brazil. We have our beaches and our pleasure in the body. But those men, lining up together to pray!'

The Brazilian told me how, when travelling, he had taken a photograph of a rather beautiful tree in the *suq* in Dongola. Someone had then tried to wrest his camera from him and he had been taken to the police station, camera intact, but he had been shaken by the experience. Ironically, it is the xenophobia of the authorities, which drives tourists away and deprives the economy of millions of dollars, that preserves Sudan as a place worth travelling in!

I had also met a daring Australian who had travelled from Juba to Kosti by barge, spending some two weeks on the Nile, coming through the swamp of the Sudd, passing the barges going in the opposite direction up river with the displaced now returning to Juba just before the referendum. Fortunately, there had been no cows on board; apparently their presence can double journey time as the cattle have to be taken on shore daily to graze.

My taxi driver turned to me. His had been a dry New Year's Eve.

'I don't drink, you know!' I expressed approval.

'And I have never been with a woman!' I suppose I should have expressed approval again, but I laughed. Abdu looked a good 30 years old, but the Sudanese, compared to other countries like Yemen where a boy might marry before he sported a moustache, tend to marry late.

'What's up then?' I asked. 'Is there something wrong with the equipment?' He laughed.

'It's a matter of circumstances. Getting a job here is not about qualifications. Here, you have to be one of the National Congress.

I knew the story; this discrimination certainly wasn't something unique to Karima. Karima had its dam and its bridge and its new hospital, but although the Shayqiyya are one of the politically dominant groups in Sudan, part of the *aulad al baher*, I certainly wasn't overwhelmed by a sense of development. In *Season of Migration to the North*, a villager from this neglected part of Sudan protests at the policies that had bought the development of Khartoum at the expense of the rest of the country: 'Aren't we human beings? Don't we pay taxes? Haven't we any rights in this country? Everything's in Khartoum. The whole of the country's budget is spent in Khartoum.'[3] That was in the 1960s. What would the author have said about the past two decades?

'I have only my secondary school education.'

'And what is a university education now worth? I mean those guys in Khartoum graduate and then drive a rickshaw if they're lucky.' In the past 20 years, 'universities', many of them private, had mushroomed all over the North.

'How many universities are there now in Sudan? Fifty.'

'Fifty?'

'Fifty? Far more!'

'In Ireland we have ten or so!'

Once, when I had arrived in Shendi and asked the taxi driver to take me to the hotel where I would spend the night, he turned to me and told me that the *laconda* was now a university. Imagine the equivalent in Ireland.

'Can you take me to Sea View Bed and Breakfast on the promenade?'

'Where have you been? Sea View's now the university.'

Shendi is the nearest town to the third kingdom of Kush: Meroe. Years before I had dutifully gone there to do the sites, walking across the sands with a lad who was waiting for his lorry to pick up some spare parts. I had savoured a landscape of decapitated tombs and tombs cemented over, and caught in the far distance the green hints of the Nile. When we finally found the elderly gaffer, there was a fumbling for a key under a stone and a wooden door into a tomb was opened. Where a boat had been carved in the stone he would point his finger and say in English 'boat'; where there was a six-foot-high cow he would point his finger and say 'cow'. The rest was silence.

When I look back on that trip it is not the pyramids but the aesthetics of the gaffer's home that I remember: the woven circle of the prayer mat on the sandy floor; the hanging goatskin of cool water; the *tambour* that would intoxicate the mind in the coolness of the night suspended on the stone wall. I also remember my companion's comment as we walked across the sands. Viewing the pyramids, he had a strange sense of history.

'Why did the *khawajas* build their houses so far from the Nile?'

That was some time ago. To be fair, with the changes in the education system in the past two decades, many more Sudanese now have access to university, but the quality of what is achieved is questionable. A lawyer can graduate with an elementary level of English. The issue is not just tertiary education, but what went before. I turned to Abdu.

'And all the jobs are in Khartoum!'

'I've only ever been there twice!'

As we passed through the palm plantations, the dried leaves of other years falling against their trunks, it didn't seem to me that Abdu was missing out on much. As the Sudanese themselves say, what with the traffic and the heat, 'Khartoum! Khartoum! It's just hassle!'

In the west, travel has become an obsession. In Sudan, it is a very different matter; there are the traditional movements of nomads as they follow the rhythms of the year in search of pasture; then there are the well-off who like to holiday in Egypt. A more typical reason for travel is to escape conflict: you are not so much a traveller as displaced.

There is not a lot of curiosity about what lies beyond the home town. While the Australian might travel the length of the African continent and beyond, the Sudanese lads I had met the day before in the *suq* were fairly indifferent to their own country. One from Kordofan had been half a dozen years in Karima, yet he had never got on the bus and travelled two hours down the road to check out Dongola. And one of my trainees from East Sudan had lived a year in Blue Nile State before he made it down to the Nile, just a ten minute walk from class. My driver, too, sensed a difference in outlook.

'Maybe this year I'll have a son. And I'll call him Richard after you in the hope that he will have your brains!'

'That would be nice. My brains, and your body!'

Indeed, the dominant tribe in the region, the Shayqiyya, are a splendid lot, with the women still wearing the traditional *tobe* and the men still donning the traditional white *jelabiyah*, or *arraqi* and *sirwal*. Such is the intensity of the heat, the material from which the loose *arraqi* that hangs over the *sirwal* trousers is made is almost translucent. The people often have a lovely *asmer* complexion. *Asmer* is a colour for which I can think of no word in English; it is the same reddish-brown, with hints almost of copper, of the figures that decorate the tombs of antiquity in the area. Shayqiyya beauty was not wasted on Waddington, who travelled with a connoisseur's appreciation of life, writing for example that crocodile meat 'a little resembles scrimped skate'. In a footnote he adds: 'The Shayqiyya … are black, a clear, glossy, jet-black, which appeared, to my then unprejudiced eyes, to be the finest colour that could be selected for a human being.'[4] They were so black they shone.

The Shayqiyya were the most warlike tribe in North Sudan. At the time of Waddington's travels, the Turks under Ismail Pasha were attempting to subdue the tribe, who, armed with crocodile skin shields and charms to protect themselves, went into battle as if it were a game. According to tradition, the signal to attack would have been given by a beautiful virgin on a camel, and the men would go to, greeting the enemy with '*Salaam aleikoum!*' as if meeting long lost friends.[5] The peace they intended to bring, however, was the peace of death. In the Battle of Korti, the Shayqiyya charms did not work before Turkish guns and it was the Shayqiyya warriors who encountered peace. Waddington writes that Ismail Pasha offered 50 piastres for each human ear presented, and 3,000 human ears — not necessarily from the dead — were delivered to his father in Cairo 'as proofs of his successes'.[6]

Today amulets are popular, but not everyone approves of such things. As he drove, I touched Abdu's *jelabiyah* above the biceps and it seemed to me that he was wearing something beneath the sleeve.

'What's this, Abdu? It's not an amulet, is it?'

'I'm a Muslim. We don't wear amulets.'

As I had walked back from Jebbel Berkel in the darkness of New Year's Eve I had heard the rhythms of a Sufi celebration coming from within the walls of a house.

'The Sufis? I suppose they are not bad, but...' Before he could express his disapproval, we arrived at Nuri. For me Nuri was a place of palms and Nile-watered aubergine fields, but for archaeologists, Nuri has a greater significance.

The Egyptians may have brought their religion to Jebbel Berkel, but in a much later era the Sudanese extended their Kingdom of Kush to embrace Egypt. The twenty-fifth dynasty, known as the Nubian Dynasty or the Kushite Empire (760–656 BC), was a Sudanese one, with the Kushite kingdom extending as far as Alexandria. The pyramid of Taharqo is to be found in Nuri, and a black sphinx, 'the Sphinx of Taharqo', is to be found in the British Museum in London. The sphinx is unquestionably the image of an African pharaoh.[7]

The British Museum's director, Neil MacGregor, speaks of a cultural fault line between Egypt and Sudan that has reflected a cultural divide for millennia. But perhaps that fault line, today at least, actually falls more to the south of Khartoum, somewhere around the latitude of Malakal perhaps? It's tempting for someone like me to feel that the Muslim Sudanese have more in common with Egyptians than they have with Southern Sudanese.

Amulet

'So are you telling me those men in Kordofan wearing amulets are not Muslims?'

'What will they do for you? Do you wear them?'

I must confess I rather liked the amulets, the sensuality of dark leather against *asmer* skin. But Abdu was talking on ideological terms, and Irish Presbyterians, focusing on the Word rather than on other rituals, do not much go in for such things either.

'No, we're like you. We don't do that sort of thing. And the Sufis? What do you think of the Sufis, Abdu?'

Traditional life, Nuri

In Nuri that day, the *suq* had the life of a market day, with the buzz of conversation and the fruit displayed on the stalls. People still squatted on the ground to share a dish of *fuul* beans together and indolently lingered on in the cafés. I handed over two 10 Sudanese pound notes to Abdu, with their image of the Republican Palace on one side and the mountains of Kassala on the other. Abdu's response was not an unusual one in Sudan – the appeal for smaller notes.

'I haven't got any change!' It's a phrase I've heard a thousand times since my first days in Sudan. But this was not an attempt to add a tip to the fare; Abdu handed one of the Sudanese ten pound notes back to me. I then returned it to him. After all the haggling at the beginning of the journey, it seemed that money was not an issue now.

That evening we met up by chance again in the *suq*. I was tired and irritable from walking around all day in the intense heat in pursuit of images of villagers among palms, for not a lot has changed in these Nile landscapes which the novelist loved, even though the Nile steamer dislodging its passengers may now just be a memory. The light that day had been as intense as the heat, and those shots suggesting the old ways that had almost disappeared had evaded me. The local baker had offered fresh bread and the lads cutting the dead leaves of the palms had been affable enough, but the wide sandy beach by the Nile, despite it being the heart of winter, had been insufferably hot. That evening, the tea woman was graceless and slow, and I did not much take to Abdu's companions. It was not just the heat that had tired me; I was tired of all the endless Sudanese talk. Talk, talk, talk… Do they never, ever stop talking?

The next day I would suffer the bus journey back to Khartoum with hours of singers accompanied by an electric organ. The days of Bob Marley sounding out had gone, although many a lad still sports a skull-cap with Jamaican/Ethiopian colours. If it were not a jolly electric organ filling the hours, the music on the bus would be a group singing sanctimonious sludge. In the case of New Year's Day in Karima however, it was the journey to Nuri and not the destination that mattered.

NOTES

1 Moorehead, Alan, *The Blue Nile* (Penguin Books, 1983) p.175
2 Waddington, George, *Journal of a Visit to Some Parts of Ethiopia* (London: John Murray, 1822) p.159
3 Salih, op. cit. p.118
4 Waddington, op. cit. p.122
5 Waddington, op. cit. p.98
6 Waddington, op. cit. p.174
7 MacGregor, Neil, *A History of the World in 100 Objects* (Penguin, 2010) p.141

CHAPTER EIGHT

BRAVE NEW WORLD

FLYING TO JUBA

The Khartoum sky was hinting of rain as I was dropped off at the *Hajj* and *Umra* section of the airport. I was not doing the pilgrimage but on my way to Juba, a city which is in some ways the antithesis of things Islamic. In the airport entrance the x-ray machine was out of order, and a mass of passengers gathered around it with an array of cases, bags and cardboard boxes; the Sudanese do not travel light.

In the airport lounge things were not much better: the electricity was on but the air-conditioning was off and the temperature must have been 40 degrees. But someone I had met once or twice, Dinka-tall and dressed in jacket and tie, handed me a bottle of cool water. Majok[1] had just left his university post in Malakal, and was all set to move to Juba.

'So you'll be teaching in Juba University?'

'My brother has a money exchange place. I'll be working there.' I doubted, however, if his departure from Malakal was just a matter of university politics, for these days people were tending to rejoin their own ethnic group.

I had once worked in Malakal, teaching civil servants in a tin-roofed, mud-walled room by the radio station. It had been the usual scenario: appalling facilities, delightful trainees. The town stank from the sewage brought to the surface in the rains and a tent proved much better than a shared house in town.

Hygiene in Malakal left something to be desired. Even at the bakery flies congregated on the cow hides hung out to dry and in the cafés flies would land on my glass of tea before it reached my lips. At the side of the road, men were sitting idly outside the grocer's with the pot of *fuul* simmering away, and a yard in front of them was the fetid ditch. Couldn't they get a shovel and clear it?

175

Malakal at the time seemed a laid-back place to me, and in some *rokuba* I'd idle hours away over coffee, chatting with the soldiers. In the late afternoon, the men would congregate by the river, where the phrase 'Joint Units' appeared in a different light. A couple of months after I had left, elements of the Joint Units, units from both SAF and SPLA brought together to enforce the peace agreement, fought it out, turning on each other. In the resulting conflict, hundreds were killed and the University was looted. I had been in Syria, but Majok had been in Malakal when it had all happened.

'I was there at the time. They nearly killed me!' Majok, being Dinka Bor, would have been in the minority in the Shilluk– and Nuer–dominated town.

'They took everything. My clothes, my equipment... They took everything but my books.'

'They'd have no interest in those, I'm sure!'

'My supervisor was out from Norway. She was hospitalized for a week afterwards.'

'Was she injured?'

'Shock!'

Up in Khartoum, ordinary people use the blanket term 'Southerners' to refer to very diverse ethnic groups. Apart from those who had fought there in the war, the South was this uniformly unknown place, like one of those maps in Renaissance times where unexplored parts were marked with 'Here be Dragons!' Even one of the streetwise rickshaw drivers, on hearing where I lived in Khartoum, said with amazement:

'But there are Nuer there!' Another driver mocked him.

'Watch out, Richard! There are LIONS in the street where you live!' The lions were squatting in the empty plots that would become the next high-rise apartment blocks, pastoralists whose children had probably never seen a cow.

Among Southern Sudanese there were huge ethnic divisions. The war was repeatedly referred to as being between the 'Arab-Islamic North' and the 'African-Christian South', a massive oversimplification, especially as some Southern ethnic groups had sided with Khartoum against the Dinka-dominated SPLA that was fighting to free the South from 'Arab'-Muslim rule.

If such divisions lay within the Southern Sudanese themselves, what about the 'Arab' Sudanese who ran the grocery shops in Malakal? What would be their place in the new South? They had been charming to me when I bought my groceries and I feared what might happen to them in the coming days.

At last our flight was called. The pilot did his religious bit as we cruised for take-off. He couldn't

Traditional markings in Malakal

just say his verses privately; it had to be broadcast to the entire plane, although we were, after all, flying to Juba not Mecca.

Majok had showed me the website on his laptop with the referendum countdown timed in seconds. I doubted if people would wait, feeling that it was people with guns who decide the course of history, not citizens voting in referendums. In this I was proved wrong and the referendum went ahead in a very credible way.

Majok pointed out of the window; I had not been very observant. Two massive planes were preparing for take-off, with troops marching around one of them. SAF forces were entering the great belly of the plane.

'They're off to Darfur!' I turned to Majok.

'I heard on *Al Jazeera* that over 300 were killed in Darfur last week.'

'Yes, it's true.'

'Darfur! Is it the South: Part Two?' In the intimacy of the plane, I now had the opportunity to check out one or two things.

'As a foreigner, as an outsider, it seems to me that the South was about… Well, first of all it was about "Arabization". And secondly it was Islamization. And of course – and maybe this is number one – it was about oil.'

Majok raised no objection to this view of the conflict.

'And Darfur? Well, it's Arabization again. And of course there's the oil. But they can't claim Islamization this time round, can they? The Fur are Muslims.' In a sense there has however been a kind of 'Islamization' in that ideologies that reflect a much more legalistic interpretation of Islam have played their part in Darfur with its more Sufi-orientated Islam. Majok was still focused on the South:

'But you forgot the minerals. When you think of all that we have in the South, they had the right to attack us!'

'How can you say that!'

'Well, not a right, but it made sense.'

'And after separation in South Sudan you will have two sources of revenue: oil and aid. How are you going to export your oil, if not through the North?'

There was talk of a pipeline to Mombasa, but this would make the South dependent on Kenya rather than Khartoum. The reality was that the South currently had very limited sources of revenue. I turned to my fellow passenger.

'Let's consider the dream scenario. Borders are agreed. The referendum is fair. And the North agrees to separation. And then the two separate states agree to continue trading together. Now what are the chances of that happening? And what about South Kordofan?'

'The people there will decide.'

South Kordofan, with its oil fields and ethnic diversity, was likely to be an area of further conflict. Even the issue of who would have the right to vote in border areas like Abyei had not been resolved; as in that Genesis myth of Cain and Abel, the settled were in conflict with the nomadic.

A breakfast of cheese omelette and sausages was served by Egyptian stewards as Majok told me about his time doing his Master's in Scandinavia.

'I told them I would die there from the winter!'

'And the people? Were they interested in Sudan?'

'Very!'

'I've never understood that Norwegian interest in South Sudan. I mean, the British with their history, of course. And the Americans. But the Norwegians, how do you explain their interest?'

'I can't.'

'Does it begin with O and end with an L by any chance?'

We were now nearing Juba. I could see the Nile and swampy lakes and the occasional cluster of huts. Our approach seemed a leisurely one. It had not been like this in the past! Planes had flown high until Juba and then descended almost vertically in a corkscrew to avoid being fired on.

'And in the war, how long did the SPLA hold Juba for?'

'They had the surrounding areas. But the town? Just in the last days.'

We taxied to a halt, just outside the tiny airport building. It was a sunny day, with touches of white cloud, and temperatures just in the mid-20s. A banner hung across the wire where we entered the airport building. 'Vote for secession! Stand up for secession!' I turned to Majok.

'That looks like a message from the grassroots!' He seemed to approve.

'It's the young people here! They are not free to do this in Khartoum!'

'It looks as if their views are a bit different from those at the top!'

Luggage took an eternity and my driver didn't turn up, but there were taxis at the main entrance. I wasn't sure what language to use with a taxi driver in Juba.

'Would you prefer English or Arabic?'

'I have both, but I prefer English.'

'And what's your name?'

'Matata-safi!' I had picked up a few words of Swahili years before when I had travelled in Kenya, fleeing Sudan during the Gulf War.

same, while others bathed devoid of the garments required in Khartoum.

I was with Adam, a colleague originally from Darfur, down from Khartoum for the first time. We greeted the soldiers on the bailey bridge and, given the picturesque view, Adam reminded me of the camera in my backpack. I had been too long in Sudan for that.

'If I take a shot of the Nile, they'll say I'm photographing the bridge.'

'But haven't they heard of Google Earth?'

Villagers, one with a goat, were walking across in single file. For a city, Juba was a very rural place. On first arriving in Juba Town I was amazed at the 'city' I found. Juba proper was just like those small towns found in East Africa with their tin-roofed buildings and verandas functioning as hardware stores or groceries. Why would anyone fight for two decades over such a place? But in Juba it's not what's on the surface but what lies beneath the ground that matters.

Some of the displaced were still camped out in the street near the mosque, gathering around fires to cook some porridge or gruel with the tarpaulins under which they slept hanging from the shop balconies. Not without a sense of guilt, I'd walk past them to the nearby bar in the evenings, a bar managed by two Greek-Sudanese brothers.

'*Matata* is Swahili, isn't it? And *safi*? Is that Swahili as well as Arabic? So were you born in Kenya?'

'No here, in Yea.' My driver's English hinted of education abroad.

'But you went to school in Uganda?'

'In our tradition, the parents name the child after the situation in which it *was* born.' We laughed at that. And so, with an employee of the Ministry of Information, now moonlighting, I rode into Juba town with Pure Problem as my driver. So that had been the situation at the time of his birth: nothing but problems.

THE VIEW FROM JUBA BRIDGE

The rains had come, the afternoons building up with a cloudy heat until teaching was silenced as rain thundered on roofs. That to me is the sound of Africa: rain on tin roofs.

The Nile at Juba Bridge was not a disappointment. The waters at this time of year were a rich brown and water hyacinths were clogging together against the pillars of the bridge. On the riverbank, generators pumped up water for the lads washing down Land-cruisers. Under a tree, someone openly smoked a joint. Further along the banks men congregated to do the

Juba, the view from the hotel

Juba street scene: Ugandan residents working as dobymen

One night, as I made my way to the bar through Juba's darkening streets, Puccini was sounding out luxuriantly from the sound system. When I was a young volunteer in Malawi I could never have imagined myself in this situation: avoiding the utterly destitute in the street, the mothers settling down on some squalid mat with their children, as I made for a wood-fired pizza and a couple of beers in a stylish bar. Juba is the first and third worlds brought together – or rather kept distinctly apart – all in a couple of streets.

As an aid worker in Juba you can have a good time. The west portrays itself as altruistic in what it does in Africa, and aid workers are cast in some kind of angelic role. When I revisited the Belfast school I had left for my first stint in Africa, an elderly colleague asked if I had 'heard the call'! The reality, in terms of repayments of international loans for example, is anything but altruism, and the aid industry has its fair share of pleasure-seekers, an altogether healthier situation, perhaps, than suffering angels.

It's life without the normal responsibilities. Almost no one is there with their family and, in the upper ranks of the industry, especially if you are with the Gravy Train, there are generous *per diems* to spend or save as you like. And it is not only the expats who enjoy the *per diems*. The aid industry was producing a strange

mentality in Juba. Some trainees resented getting free language training during working hours in their own Ministry. Why weren't they being trained in Dar as Salaam or Nairobi, with the generous *per diems* that this would bring?

Juba is not a place for the bland. Seated at the bar would be a former British officer now running a private security firm. It was his off-hand comment that gave me the best insight into what Khartoum's policies of Arabization and Islamization had meant for the South. Recruiting men of the right age was a problem for his firm in Juba.

'After the war, we can't get young men in their twenties or early-thirties. There are hardly any left alive to recruit.' And then turning to the Kenyan barman:

'Any sign of that pizza we ordered?'

Then there was his Irish companion, knocking back yet another beer, organising literacy programmes for adults in the villages, nipping in the bud any aid-dependence mentality.

'I told them that if they wanted a school in their village, they had better get started and build it!'

With us was a Kenyan woman who was much more on the ball than some expat just flown in from Europe or the USA. As they had done in Khartoum in the 1990s, so in Juba they, too, were throwing out the

Notos Bar, Juba

baby with the bath water, but this time it was the utter rejection of Arabic for English.

'How can they reduce the number of teachers! They are dismissing the ones trained in the Arabic pattern. They need to be retrained, not sacked!' This was the world I would enjoy for a couple of months.

A few minutes had been enough to cross Juba Bridge. Now, at its end, a truck driver was discussing something with the men at the checkpoint; negotiating a bribe perhaps? Beyond was a sea of roofs, which Adam christened Zinc Town. It was the roadside mêlée of the equivalent of a service station, with one shack even promising banking services. The White Nile flowed darkly beneath us and Adam contemplated our distance from Khartoum.

'If we were in a boat, how long would it take us to reach Khartoum?'

'Floating down? What do you think?'

'A month?'

I would have thought less. But for those Victorian explorers of the Nile, going upriver from Khartoum, progress often came to an end in the fetid swamps of the Sudd. One British hunter, having arrived in Omdurman in 1901, wrote of his later travels in the Sudd. There was the silence that came with the absence of life, feasting mosquitoes excepted, as the boat passed through 'an endless avenue of papyrus, tall and slender and of a most perfect green', their journey marked by the sickly-sweet smell of rotting vegetation.[2] The Sudd, the South's natural barrier, had allowed traditional ways of life to continue beyond the reach of advancing commerce.

Ironically, the conflict which had killed two million Southern Sudanese had also made the South, for the aid worker Emma McClune, a place apart. Emma opted to live in a hut in a guerrilla camp with the guerrilla leader she had married as his second wife. For her it was an Eden, sealed off from the rest of the world by war.[3] Now, with apparent peace, all that was set to change; with all those oil reserves Juba apparently had the potential to become one of the richest pieces of real estate in the world.[4] As international companies competed to get their hands on that oil, English-language programmes and school projects, packaged as aid, would help to serve their needs. Teachers such as I were part of the advancing frontier of westernization that would transform the lands of the pastoralists into real estate.

The Nile in Sudan is like an old familiar friend you meet in unfamiliar places, but here even the Nile seemed different. Strictly speaking, we were viewing not so much the White Nile as one of its tributaries.

The waters seemed to move purposely forward, directly, unlike the great leisurely sweeps of the Blue Nile before the White Nile joins it at Khartoum. The Northern capital already seemed another country, but one thing, however, was just the same: a thick-set man in a track suit challenged us in badly pronounced English.

'What are you doing on the bridge?' His manner was less than charming and the explanation 'Enjoying the view' was not going to work.

Tourism has not yet taken off in Juba, although it has a thriving equivalent: the aid industry workers staying in a variety of hotels with rates that might rival New York's. And Juba has its own distinctive architecture. Most of the hotels are a series of containers, such as you see stacked at a port. A night in such a container, the rings to which the former cargo was once tied still authentically remaining on the walls, could easily set you back US$100, breakfast of bacon and sausages included.

Customer-care for two stakeholders in the South Sudan tourist industry seemed to be a little lacking as our man in the tracksuit harangued us.

'Get off the bridge! Don't stand here!'

As Juba has its own debased form of Arabic so it has its own variety of English in which the polite forms such as 'would you' and 'could you' are noticeably lacking. As it is in the military, so it is in civilian life: imperatives abound! I would also have to revise that view Churchill had of the North as the Military Sudan; the South was mirroring it perfectly. Perhaps the man who had confronted me in Omdurman *Suq* was right after all: 'All Sudan is a military area'. We walked back, feigning nonchalance.

'What are you going to have back in the hotel? A nice, cold Tusker beer?'

Back on the Bridge Hotel terrace we sat beneath massive mango trees. The terrace was tastefully paved, the restaurant carefully thatched, the waitresses stylishly-dressed Ethiopians. I turned to Adam.

'You guys are asleep in Khartoum! Couldn't you do something like this, even if it was just for coffee?'

'There was a time when Ugandans flew from Kampala to Khartoum for a weekend in its bars!'

From the hotel terrace, we watched the light soften over Nile waters. A lone boatman was casting his circular net, a net that I have seen used from the seas off Suakin to the islands of Yemen. He pulled a Nile perch into his dugout canoe with ease and bystanders on the terrace offered to purchase the catch. A genial bargaining ensued. The waters and the sky merged so that the distant hills misted over.

Some Juba elders were sitting at a nearby table. Dress is a strange thing in Juba. In town, some spoke of former days when tribesmen had walked the streets naked; today, men on the make, more British than the British, opt for heavy western suits, totally unsuitable for the climate. For late afternoon refreshments on the hotel terrace, however, these elders in their thick glasses were wearing pyjamas with a paisley motif, a return to the original function of pyjamas: daywear in a hot climate.

At the next table, a few guys 'here on business' had been sipping orange juice. One was from the Nuba Mountains, another from Darfur. As they paid their bill, one explained:

'I'm just going to have a shower and then get dressed.' He smiled knowingly and I understood.

'Well, make sure you take something to wear for protection as well!'

On the far bank, the trees were speckled with roosting egrets, fidgeting from branch to branch as the dusk thickened. Frogs began their chorus as mosquitoes gathered in swarms. With darkness, our driver took us back.

'After dark, you don't want to be on Juba roads! Robbers beat up pedestrians and strip them of their possessions. And the police shift ends before midnight!'

Terrace by the White Nile, Juba

I wondered what effect the exit of the police would have on the ambience of the city streets.

'And then there are the checkpoints! They stopped me and asked, "Have you any guns?" They accused me of immoral behaviour because I had a woman in the car. I was taking my wife to hospital!'

He dropped us at De Havana Bar, where the men drinking were politeness itself, giving us their table for us to eat our pizza. They looked as if they were dressed for the office, not for a night out, but one sat in beach-shorts

Tucked away in a little space on the last page I noticed something about a military leader who had broken away and was fighting South Sudan troops. Adam explained.

'He was high up in the military. His name's George Athor Deng.'

'Deng! So he's Dinka and he's fighting SPLA troops! I don't believe it!' This was a new one for me: a Dinka 'renegade general' fighting against those who had liberated the South. As a man at the bar once explained, here everyone wants to be *beng*, the Big Boss.

'He stood for election and didn't get the result he expected.' Apparently George Athor had run for Governor of Jonglei State as an independent candidate and lost. Had the election been unfair? For me there was a broader issue.

'If he's in the military, what was he doing standing for election anyway?'

An 'international' group had now gathered at the bar. De Havana is where expatriates would come for salsa, but it was not just the expats. There were Sudanese present who had travelled in the west but had never been to Khartoum. At the bar, 'lost boys' – a misnomer if there ever was one, for the 'lost boy' would be six foot six and built like an athlete – would tell me their stories. With the destruction of their villages and

with his arm hanging carelessly over his mate's shoulders. In Juba, where the Guinness is a fruity 6 per cent alcohol, they drink! But there isn't usually the aggression that is released on weekend streets in Ireland. If anything, I found some of the Sudanese in Juba rather abrasive during the day but often pleasantly mellow after a few drinks.

The World Cup was playing on the big screen and Abba, as ever, sounded out over the sound system. Women in wigs and the briefest of skirts sat together; Auntie Betty with her hair up for church but with the clinging mini of the rapper's chick. Often women would arrive after 11.00pm, starting the evening after the men had already tanked up and their judgement was somewhat impaired. One woman in a scarlet dress sat down between us and the men from Juba. I found it a bit hard to take, prudish after all those years in Khartoum; the woman directly opposite was not exactly hiding her wares. It was a far cry from the North, but Adam seemed not so much dumbfounded as amused.

A free newspaper was being distributed and I wondered, given all the evangelical forces at work in the region, if it was not the South Sudan equivalent of the Salvation Army's *War Cry*. The paper was political, however, the headline warning against warmongering.

the killing of their families, they had found refuge in Ethiopia where they received 'schooling'.

That's the official version. According to the author of *Emma's War*, 'lost boys' was a misnomer for a quite different reason: they weren't 'lost' war orphans at all but child conscripts, pawns in a complicated war game. I heard from a 'lost boy' who had lived in a training camp in Ethiopia, how, if any kind of inspection from an international team was due, the training camp was set up to look like the boys were attending classes. The camps of 'lost boys' were a source of Gravy Train aid, the aid often going to feed the boys' 'caretakers', not the boys.[5] Now, decades later, after schooling in Kenya followed by refuge in Cuba or Canada or Australia, the 'lost boys' were back home, knocking back shots at the bar, flamboyantly dressed, larger than life and investing in South Sudan with their lives.

The bar was now filling up. Unlike in Khartoum, people in Juba know how to have a good time. If you have money you spend it; if you don't you spend someone else's. The waitress, modestly dressed, brought another Kenyan Tusker beer.

'Do you think she's Sudanese?'

'No, I'd say she's Kenyan.' Almost all the staff were industrious Kenyans or Ugandans. In Juba I was more likely to pick up Swahili than, say, the language of the indigenous Bari ethnic group. As in some oil-rich Gulf states it was foreigners in Juba who did the work.

Not one of the tankers I saw filling up with water to be delivered to homes was driven by a Sudanese; I was told such work was stigmatized. Meanwhile, as work that did not seem particularly specialized was done by workers from other African countries, a lot of young men seemed to be spending their days with their feet up, reclining in a chair, watching the world go by. Did they really see such work as beneath them? Or, in that wonderful Gravy Train catch-all term, did they need some 'capacity-building' in order to fill up a tanker with water?

As footballers posed on the massive screen before the next match, nearer the bar we were getting the full run of Abba hits as the singer called out that she was the first in line and still free. Take a chance on me! I was back in the Grand in Khartoum again, musically at least, for McCulture was embracing us all. I wondered just how free it all was. As the dream of a separate Southern state seemed about to become a reality, I felt that people were likely to confuse independence and freedom. Just as the North was dominated by the *awlad al baher*, would the South, too, be dominated by one or two ethnic groups?

Ugandan resident, Juba

And if you were a woman in South Sudan, what did 'freedom' mean? Among my trainees there were talented women who would forge a professional career in the new South; I was lucky to have taught such women at such a time. But in the bars, freedom for women — and they were nearly all women from Kenya or Uganda — seemed to mean hooking a man for a commercial transaction.

When you say 'Juba' in Khartoum, the Sudanese respond as if you were talking about a place of unrestricted pleasure. If you were an unattractive, middle-aged, white male in search of a female for the night, perhaps it was. I saw half a dozen military men from Europe arrive together, appear to drink soft drinks, get up to dance and pull within a few minutes.

It was time to turn in, although sleep would not come easy with the *vuvuzela* horns of the World Cup sounding out into the early hours. Juba certainly was a world apart from the Sudan I knew; culturally it was much closer to Kenya and Uganda than to Khartoum. Was there anything, apart from conflict, that united Khartoum and Juba? The two cities were poles apart, but were similar in that they were both extreme. In one city it was not unusual for a woman to wear socks and gloves, despite the intense heat, rather than expose the flesh. In the other, it didn't seem as if many at the bar — one evening over 1,000 had come to De Havana for drink and music — were setting out to 'keep the promise'. I turned to my colleague.

'Adam, I think there might, after all, be something to be said for the North and the *tobe*!'

AT THE QUEEN'S BIRTHDAY PARTY

It was the Sudanese speaker who called on everyone gathered to stand for the national anthems. We waited with our glasses in hand, the cucumber and carrot dips on a tray on the table, but someone had forgotten, by accident I'm sure, to set up the music. They're always an embarrassment anyway, national anthems.

The British ambassador gave the perfect speech, seemingly off the cuff, ironic, brief. The Sudanese speaker, however, set out to tick a lot of boxes.

There was the quotation from the first Queen Elizabeth about a tiny nation defending itself from invasion. Then he gently chided those NGOs who, fearing the worst, had left the country before the elections.

'South Sudan is not like the Congo or Nigeria or Kenya; here, there is an exemplary tolerance of other ethnic groups.' Obviously we had been reading different newspapers.

'South Sudan is a new thing in Africa!'

Waitress in a bar in Juba

Indeed. The emerging state had allegedly reached levels of corruption that other African states had taken 50 years to cultivate. I heard that so much aid money was being siphoned off it was contributing to the escalation of house prices in Nairobi.

The relationship between Sudan and the UK was further explored, as the speaker delved back a century-and-a-half to when a British explorer and his wife-to-be (Baker later married his mistress) had travelled here. Strangely enough, I had met a Ugandan called Samuel Baker that very afternoon, hawking a mirror and suitcases around the streets of Juba with his two sons, searching not for the source of the Nile but a customer.

The speaker moved on.

'It is Britain's duty to clean up the mess it has created!' More than half a century after their departure, it was the colonialists, not the indigenous leadership, who were held responsible for the state of Sudan. Were the Sudanese leadership, Kipling-like, still calling on Britain to 'take up the white man's burden'? Our speaker had to compete with the ever-increasing chat that was coming from the crowd, who thankfully were more interested in the wine that was now on tap than responding to Kipling's invitation. But there was one more thorny issue to refer to: the referendum.

Pothole problems, Juba town

'Five years is not a long time, but Unity has been made attractive! Just look at the roads, and schools, and health facilities that have been built!' Was the speaker a master of irony? The roads in Juba seemed to lead to the private mansions of the blessed, those who were 'building the nation', and although Juba had a casino, I couldn't find a basic government health clinic.

Up in Khartoum they were still assuming Unity; why would the South want to break away? A Sudanese doctor I met returning briefly to Khartoum from his life abroad had more of a sense of things. He told me how a friend had put it: 'If those slaves want to break away, we'll let them go.'

The language says it all really. For that travelled doctor (it feels at times that there are more Sudanese doctors in Dublin and London than in Khartoum) the conflict was essentially about race and ethnicity. Who could disagree with that? But there was a third factor, linked to the first two: Islamism. If Sudan were an Islamic state, by definition any Christian was a second-class, though theoretically protected, citizen and anyone animist was something beneath that again.

The words displayed above the reception in the New Sudan Palace Hotel said it all: 'Why should I want to be a second-class citizen in someone else's state when I could be a first-class citizen in my own country?'

Those were the words, half-remembered here, of Garang, apparently giving his blessing on separation if that was the people's choice. But the hotel itself showed the folly of those who spoke in simplistic terms of an Islamic North and a Christian-animist South. Here in 'the Christian-animist South' the owner was hosting Ramadan break-fasts in the hotel garden for Juba dignitaries.

The complexities of Sudan defy description; what history there is in just one man's name, when the first is a Christian name like Peter, the second an indigenous name from his tribe and the third a Muslim name like Abdullah? What pigeon-hole does he fit into?

But as the referendum approached, North and South seemed to be on different planets. Up in Khartoum they were in their usual state of denial. A rather solid monument – a map of all Sudan – had suddenly appeared in Mak Nimer Street, with the words 'Our strength is in our Unity' emblazoned below the map in Arabic.

Meanwhile in Juba, one of my trainees had brought the words of the proposed new national anthem to class. We dished out the copies and he sat there, his cheeks cut up in what he claimed was a motorbike accident but which had all the marks of a punch-up. The anthem began with a reference to God, of course. It then went on to address the 'great warriors' of the nation, remembering the 'two million martyrs' whose blood cemented the foundation of the state. We were heading, apparently, for a land of milk and honey, inhabited by hardworking youth.

In the dreams of the proposed national anthem, I was living it seems, not in Juba with its shanty towns and straggling suburbs like *Utla burra* (Get out of here!) but in the land of Kush, 'the first civilisation in the world'. Kush? I had travelled through those Kushite kingdoms by the Nile way north of Khartoum, but I had never heard of Kush extending south to Juba. Kush would be a more appropriate name for the North; perhaps the two states could swap names?

Plans were now afoot for the transformation not just of Juba but of all the cities and towns of South Sudan. Just as Dubai has its offshore man-made islands in the shape of a palm tree, so there were plans afoot to have the new city of Juba built in the form of a rhino. Other towns would be similarly themed: this one would be planned as a pineapple; that one would take the shape of a bird. In Juba, I did sometimes have a sense of living in *Animal Farm*, but this was taking the new state beyond credibility.

But at least I had the freedom to drink and not endure the rules of another's religion. I joined the men near the bar.

'And how's Khartoum?'

'I rather like the place!' I suppose no one had said this before to the civil servants of the Ministry of International Relations.

'And Juba?'

'I suppose I'm growing to like it.' There were howls of disbelief. One of the civil servants had been to the UK, a dream destination for some Sudanese.

'To do a Master's?'

'No, before that.'

'As an undergraduate?'

'No, before that! I went to school there as a refugee in '86 when the war broke out.'

'That's about when I first came to Sudan.'

We were trading places. He had gone there to escape Sudan; I had come to Africa to escape Ireland. One of the women came up to us and, as if they were more than mere friends, he touched her.

'Excuse me...' They moved slightly aside and some kind of arrangement was made for later in the evening.

'So how's that then?' I'm not sure what he expected; a round of applause perhaps? I must on this occasion have sounded particularly priggish.

'How's what?' Women as a commodity to be bought at the bar?

Tactfully moving on, my fellow drinker told me of his time in Britain.

'There was a university lecturer, an anthropologist who wrote the first study of us, who had known my grandfather. So when I was there, I went to find him.'

'And how were you received?'

'Warmly!'

I suppose any scholar now reading his anthropological work would see its discourse as colonial, but it would be interesting to compare that anthropologist's generation with the 'international community' today, with their display of Land-cruisers outside the bar, engaging not so much with the Sudanese as with themselves.

But perhaps I am being unfair. I could also contrast the manner of an American at the bar – the epitome of democratic politeness as he spoke to the barman – with some of the Sudanese drinkers who commanded the Kenyan barman as if he were a servant from a lower caste. I started to preach.

'I think that generation of colonialists maybe had an integrity that people in the aid industry don't have today.' I was, I knew, on dubious ground. Part of the South of Sudan had once been under Belgium's King Leopold II's control. A feature of what was once the Belgian Congo next door had been the numbers of Africans whose limbs had been amputated by their 'civilizing' European plantation managers.

'I agree.'

'I mean, they probably believed in what they were doing for a start.'

I was on very dubious ground. Wyndham portrays his British host in the 1930s as almost a parody of the colonial; ranting against 'the natives' and objecting to the building of Gordon College, built to educate a small Sudanese elite to serve British interests, as 'a good river site wasted'.

I suspect many of those Khartoum expats would have known only a few imperatives in Arabic. But some of those 'servants of the Crown' had been fluent speakers of Sudanese languages and genuinely interested in the culture, even if mastering the language was part of mastering the people too.

You would expect people in Sudan to vilify their former colonial rulers, but it's rare to hear it; in fact they talk about their honesty. What characterizes Thesiger's time in Sudan, however, is his doubts about his own colonial role, along with his utter respect for those whose indigenous culture was still intact though threatened by what his presence signified. About his time in Darfur he writes: 'I had no faith in the changes which we were bringing about. I craved for the past, resented the present and dreaded the future.'[6]

In contrast, most of today's aid workers could scarcely speak a word of either Arabic or any of the indigenous languages, knew next to nothing of the cultures and were doing aid on that essential fashion accessory, their Apple Mac. Livingstone had walked across the African Continent; they were driven around in Land-cruisers. Observing my fellow guests in the hotel, those advising Sudanese civil servants on national policies seemed to be the young and beautiful on their gap year. I was not alone in my scepticism.

Trees shade the banks of the Nile, Rosseires

'And it's true of "our side" today too. People like my grandfather had an integrity that our leaders don't have today!'

I would soon retire to the white cocoon next door.

It's not that the hotel was indulgent – the bedroom had the almost Spartan aesthetics of a monastery. But not a lot had changed in terms of race relations: the staff, largely Kenyan, were housed in dire conditions across the way.

Someone had run off with my wine glass. As wine on tap had now come to an end, my companion bought me a drink and disappeared in pursuit of other pleasures.

The buzz would continue into the wee hours. One morning I was woken up to the sound of gunfire, but

that was just part of the charm of staying in a 'boutique hotel' in Juba: some of De Havana's clientele were expressing their displeasure at being told to leave the bar at dawn.

NOTES

1 I have given fictional names to some people in the text.
2 Fothergill, op. cit. pp.128–9
3 Scroggins, Deborah, *Emma's War: Love, Betrayal, and Death in the Sudan* (Harper Collins, 2003) p.352
4 Ibid. p.349
5 Ibid. p.232
6 Thesiger, op. cit. p.17

CHAPTER NINE

POSTCARD FROM DARFUR

The guard waits with the pick-up; the *shamasha* kids wait in the street; we sit on plastic chairs and wait for lunch in a room with a dirt floor.

It's market day, and as we drove along the track between the women vendors with their fruit laid out on the ground, we were jammed in on all sides by the crowds, and I thought of a scene in a film such as *Proof of Life*.

Our minder orders. In true Sudanese style he does not ask what we would like to eat, but chooses for us. Smoke reeks from mutton splayed out over coals. The girl brings a mountain of meat stacked on a metal tray. We demolish most of it and the kids with the begging bowls dash for the remains in an irreverent rush. This is our day out.

★ ★ ★ ★ ★

Once we go about sunset to the place the Gravy Train frequent. Our minder and my colleague Rasheed do their prayers. I envy Rasheed that he has his prayers to look forward to. And then as we sit around the table, I watch them do some further devotion, the *tasbeeh*, miming the words of remembrance, touching the finger joints of the right hand as if telling prayer beads. Such is a night out in Nyala. It doesn't exactly make for scintillating conversation around the table! Meantime in Khartoum, rumour at work has it that I am breaching security by partying.

★ ★ ★ ★ ★

Once I almost go for a walk in the *wadi*. Our minder arrives at the rest-house and calls out.

'Mr Richard, we only have half an hour!'

199

'Half an hour?'

'We'll have lunch in that nice restaurant by the *wadi*!'

'I don't want to go for lunch in some upmarket place! It's a walk I need!' I know at times I must sound like a petulant child, but I am confined to the rest-house from 5.00pm until the driver takes me to work the next day.

'Ok, we'll have lunch here in al-Moktar then.'

Al-Moktar is where we go every day. One day I have grilled chicken, the next, for variety, I might have chicken and rice. We tend to sit within, so as not to draw too much attention to ourselves. The manager is delightful, the waiters are amusing and the food mediocre.

'That's the one place I don't want to go today!'

We drive through town, and cross the bridge: this is as far as I have ever been allowed to go in Nyala. I glimpse the flat, dry riverbed – soon those African rains will be sweeping it all clean – and the green of trees, and people gathering for their day out. We arrive at the restaurant by the *wadi*, and find it, to my relief, closed.

'I really want a walk!' We turn round and I wonder where we are going. Perhaps the *wadi* has another entrance?

There isn't a lot of conversation as we drive back through town. I soon find myself back in familiar territory: outside Al-Moktar restaurant. I get out of the pick-up – an act of rebellion! – and walk towards the rest-house. Our minder drives along, escorting me at a slight distance as I walk, until I reach the gate, where the guards sit if they are not reclining on a bed in the kitchen. I envy the swallows screeching overhead.

★ ★ ★ ★ ★

Ramadan breaks the monotony a little. The first clear sign of fasting is when I see a man kneel down in the *suq* as the vendor measures out a span of the twig with which he will clean his teeth and generate a little saliva. It's permissible to hold the traditional toothbrush in the mouth when fasting. At work they considerately bring me a flask of tea to drink in my room.

Unlike Khartoum, here in Nyala Ramadan gains momentum until the *suqs* buzz in the evenings, especially the *sheesha* dens. The Sudanese, as ever, are affability itself. But I'm confined and not free to interact.

★ ★ ★ ★ ★

Baker, Nyala

So here are my travels in Darfur. The driver picks me up from the rest-house at 8.30am. The guard sits in the back; it's like being accompanied by a fifth former with an AK47. Some days we go straight, some days we turn left. I have been living in a radius of maybe two miles – rest-house, work, shop, bakery, rest-house – for almost two months. And then it's an evening behind walls. In Ramadan I can at least sit in the street for a while over a coffee.

A soldier tells me he has been in Juba.

'And how does Nyala compare?'

'Juba was easier. Here, everything happens so quickly!'

* * * *

One Friday I have a little encounter with 'Security'. I nip down to the bus station and take some shots of the men where they sell the tickets. Flushed with success, I ask some lads selling falafel in the street near the rest-house if I can take their picture. There is something about the scene that attracts me: traditional Sudanese life, the colour.

Suddenly, someone on a motorbike is wrenching my camera from my hands. I don't let go. My personal bodyguard looks on at this, my first mugging in Sudan. The stranger pulls. I pull back, refusing to release my camera. I phone our minder and pass over the mobile. Is a *khawaja* photographing two lads selling falafel a threat to the state?

* * * *

Another time, as I leave the baker's, I stop to watch returning troops pass along the main street, a motley crew, their vehicles mounted with what I take to be rocket launchers and mounted machine guns, with missiles hanging in bags over the sides of the pickups. Their faces are often half-masked with a head-cloth as they cheer, like victorious football fans. The shoppers in the street stand to watch them pass, approving, in a way giving them the thumbs up. If these are the official troops, what are the militias like?

At last I get a sense of it: Nyala is essentially a garrison town. Outside the towns, although some tribes would have spoken Arabic, many in the rural areas would have spoken their own indigenous language. Would it be stretching things too far to see Nyala as an island of Sudanese Arabic in a sea of more indigenous languages? Perhaps.

At the bus station, Nyala

Felafel sellers, Nyala

CHAPTER TEN

SUDANS?

In Arrivals at Juba airport, there wasn't much of a sense of order and I caught the eye of another passenger.

'You know the biggest obstacle to development in this country?' he confided.

'Tell me.'

'The people themselves!' Arriving again in Juba just two months after South Sudan's independence, I connived with that genial white South African.

'And levels of corruption? How do they match other countries in Africa?'

At Immigration, however, the young official was pleasantness itself, and in a few minutes I had my visa. South Sudan was now a separate country. 'They'll be back!' they were saying in Khartoum. 'They'll be back!' Ironically, policies that had aimed to Arabize and Islamize the South, and create one Arabic speaking Islamic nation, had lost the South for Khartoum altogether.

At one level it was easy to agree with that South African, at least when it came to people at the top. The *Juba Post* for that week beginning 7 September gave a sense of the state of the nation: in Warrap State some 358 'returnees', on returning to their land of Kush, had died of starvation. According to another article, 6 billion Sudanese pounds had been 'lost' in the procurement of sorghum for emergency relief for the South. And in Juba, the indigenous Bari were apparently objecting to other ethnic groups 'grabbing land'. Incredibly, there were plans for the capital to be relocated to Lakes State in the Dinka heartlands. How could an emerging state afford a new capital? Then there was ethnic conflict in the form of 'cattle raids': a colleague in Bor had looked out of the classroom window to see the displaced fleeing tribal conflict. Over 500 had died in Jonglei that week.

Despite what was happening elsewhere, Juba did, however, have an upbeat feel and even the streets in town were clean, reflecting the pride that people had in their new country. The clock tower that had shown the countdown to independence now sported the South Sudan flag blowing in an electronic breeze. Almost unnoticed beneath was a little monument to travellers of the past: Samuel and Florence Baker, Werne, Junker… Not many in Juba, not even among the expats, would care about their lives.

I was meant to travel to Wau for work, but those African rains thundered down and the plane, although we took off, couldn't land in Wau because the runway there was flooded. I spent the time wandering in the *suqs* that pulsed with African music and life.

The Nile continued to swell and I would sit idly savouring it all, trying to remember what Conrad had written of another African river as the waters rose and flooded the terrace with the speed of an incoming tide.

A couple of days later, I was again in the departures lounge with its fake leather sofas, boarding pass for Wau in hand. The couple next to me with their child were just the kind of news that would never be in the papers; the father gorgeously tall and fine featured, gentle in the way he spoke English; the mother holding their lovely child – a family on the move.

To be more precise, they were almost on the move. When their flight to Rumbek was cancelled they just shrugged and left without complaint. And then mine was cancelled and, as ever in Sudan, I waited. If there is one text that would translate with ease into Sudanese Arabic it is *Waiting for Godot*.

I was delighted to have an extended stay in Juba, for I had never known it to be so relaxed. But elsewhere in Sudan the Comprehensive Peace Agreement was beginning to look not entirely comprehensive. Things seemed to be falling apart, or at least unravelling, and places I had travelled through were now very much in the headlines.

A few months earlier I had hung out in Cadougleh in South Kordofan, a rather lovely town in that British colonial kind of way, with its low government buildings and tree-lined streets and fringes of mud-hut villages. It had seemed idyllic; now there were reports of mass graves and fleeing civilians.

Then there was Blue Nile State, where I had recently worked. I had loved my time teaching English to the police officers there and, after classes, relaxing with the brick makers on the Blue Nile shores or idly chatting beneath shaded balconies in the *suq*. But while I was there, I heard that the SPLA would be forced to disband and leave South Kordofan. A colleague told me:

'This will be a disaster for us in Blue Nile!'

In Konda-konda Market, Juba

CHAPTER TEN: SUDANS?

Now I was beginning to see the implications. Many in South Kordofan and Blue Nile State had fought with the SPLA for a new Sudan. Now the Southern Sudanese had their own state, but they were in limbo. Could the North accommodate cultures that were neither Arab nor Islamic? As Sudan officially became more than one country, was there a chance of pluralism in the North? It looked like we would get plurality – the two Sudans – but without the pluralism that might make for a peace that could be sustained. In Blue Nile State, Sudan Armed Forces and the SPLA were again in conflict; the Governor had fled and tens of thousands of civilians were displaced. Were Blue Nile State and the Nuba Mountains of Kordofan again to become centres of major conflict?

Juba seemed a world apart from all that. By Juba Bridge they were still washing down the water tankers and I joined a few men having tea by the shacks. One explained the meaning of his name.

'It's Madol. Now that's the name of the area I'm from. But it's also our word for 'red' – that shirt he's wearing would be called *madol*. And finally, it's the colour of the bull that was sacrificed before my mother was pregnant with me.'

'You mean when you were born?'

'No, for the wedding celebrations.' He had a very natural sounding English, so I asked where he had studied.

'Under the tree! We didn't have a classroom until my first year after primary. And then I left, to fight!'

'With the SPLA?' He looked at me scathingly, and I understood.

'You are Nuer?'

He had fought with Riek Machar against Garang, whose portrait now graced the new currency of the South. I thought it prudent to pursue the topic no further, but it was incredible that anyone could have achieved such a level of language in such circumstances.

Later, as I set off to walk across Juba Bridge, someone jumped out of a minibus and greeted me. It was John Mark, whom I had known when he was a waiter, pampering us expats with carrot and ginger soup, and Kenyan coffee, then going home to study to qualify as a medical assistant. He pointed across Juba Bridge.

'I'm just coming from that side where I'm building a new *tukkul*.' He had asked me for advice when I had been a hotel guest.

'I'm thinking of getting married. Do you think it is better to marry an uneducated girl from the village who will stay at home, or marry a girl with some education who will go out to work?' I was the wrong person to give advice on marital issues, but John Mark was now building a new hut to accommodate an expanding family.

'I have a daughter now. She's two weeks old. I delivered her myself! Come back to the house to see her!'

Back in the house, a white rabbit hopped around a yard where the elders sat and chatted. John Mark and his wife and baby lived in a tiny room to themselves. She lay on the bed, holding the baby, and didn't say a word.

'I'm going to send her to school!' He was talking about the wife, not the daughter. I saw my chance for a photo of parents and child, or mother and child perhaps, but the mother stayed in the room and it was John Mark who posed with the baby. He now faced another dilemma.

'I'm not sure what to do. Should I take my own subject further? Or should I study another profession and have two?'

After I had spent these few days in Juba, that South African's comment about the people being the biggest obstacle to development wasn't holding much water. Given their circumstances, it was extraordinary what people achieved. And given the diversity of cultures, it was incredible the extent to which people managed to get on with one another.

I had been privileged to meet those people in Juba at such a time: the women from Jonglei going through the patterns for the Kordofan tailor in the *suq*; my Ugandan driver, all good nature and laughter, sharing a rented

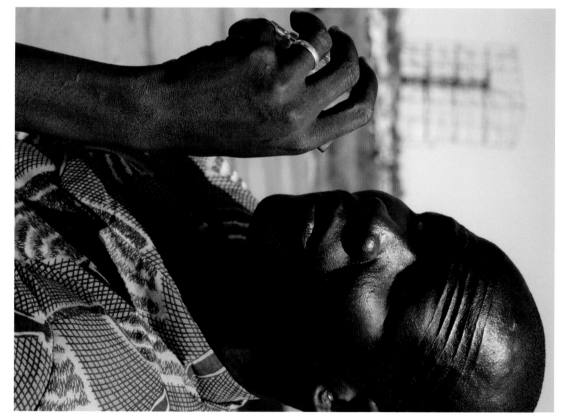

Portrait at Juba Bridge

Boda-boda drivers waiting for a fare

room with three beds with five other drivers – I rather envied him that; I was sharing mine with uninvited frogs who had entered with the rising waters; the *boda-boda* lads affably waiting on their motorbikes for a fare outside the camps; Madol with a better level of English than most university graduates in Khartoum; and John Mark, qualifying as a medical assistant as he waited on expats doing development on laptops.

Perhaps that South African had got it right when it came to those at the top. It seemed to me that the new South was beginning to mirror the North; they had learned their lessons well in Khartoum. As the South celebrated its first day of independence, the BBC had focused on the amount of land that had been signed over to multinationals. But when it comes to the grassroots, when you see those children leave some dire mud hut for school in the morning, sent out in immaculate uniforms by their mothers, you have to hope that people like these will not be betrayed.

I never did get back to Wau. After the days of waiting I was called back to Khartoum and Fred, the Ugandan driver, just got me to the airport in time. Immigration in Juba stamped my passport with an exit stamp but on arrival in Khartoum no one was interested in my passport; apparently I had never left their country. They were still in denial.

It was good to arrive in Khartoum, even though it now seemed, with so many Southerners gone, an emptier place. Those who remained, such as our institution's gardener, who had lived in Khartoum since the 1950s, having once tended the gardens of the last British Governor, seemed to have no great desire to leave, but would be happy to make a go of it in the South. But what a trainee of mine had once said about ethnicity in Sudan, something I had found ridiculous at the time, was now becoming true.

'It's like this: there are Muslim Arabs and there are foreigners.'

It looked as if Southern Sudanese would soon officially be aliens in Khartoum. We now had not just two Sudans, but two kinds of Sudanese: 'Sudanese' and 'foreigners'. This was just one of the many polarities that can be seen in Sudan. It isn't just a matter of those apparent dichotomies of Muslim and Christian, African and 'Arab'; Khartoum and Juba. Even within Khartoum there are multiple Sudans: there is the Sudan of those who drive their Land-cruisers and the Sudan of the displaced who clean them; the Sudan of those whose language is Arabic and those who express themselves in what is called a *rutaana*, and then there is the Sudan of those born and bred in Omdurman compared to those who have abandoned a pastoral life and settled in the margins.

Choosing a pattern in the *suq*

John Mark with the baby

Outside work, the lads from the Gezira were still frying up falafel and the tea ladies laughed when I pretended to pay with my new South Sudan ten-pound note. And in a ring around the charcoal stove in the intense heat of the day, the men still sat in the shade of the neem trees, talking, talking and talking.

THE MAP OF SUDAN

On Mak Nimer Street the monument of the map of Sudan is still there, but they have obliterated the South, covering it with the symbols of the diminished state that calls itself 'Sudan': the pre-Islamic pyramids of Meroe and the Shati Gate of Suakin that Kitchener had built now cover the tributaries of the White Nile – strange emblems of national identity! A massive fist clenching a spear, a dagger and a stick emboldens the North. The inscription in Arabic still reads, 'Our strength is in our Unity'.

Has partition solved any issues for the North? Within the Northern state, already a new 'South' was developing, with rebel groups, deployment of SAF troops and allegations of war crimes in Southern Kordofan. The President has promised that 'Sudan' (ie the North) will be a 'pure' Islamic state, but other Islamists, irony of ironies, are threatening to topple the government if the new constitution is not entirely based on *sharia* law. At the grassroots there's a general indifference; it's a matter of credibility, for they have heard it all before.

The issues remain the same: marginalisation; the control of the oil fields; the nature of the constitution; one interpretation of Islam being imposed on all. With open rebellion in Southern Kordofan and simmering conflict in Blue Nile State, the Popular Defence Force that was a feature of the 'jihad' against the South has been revived, and the President has promised his supporters that they will 'pray in Kudor', an area in South Kordofan held by rebels. The verb was not randomly chosen.

I've been doing a course with journalists. One trainee apologized for arriving late for class; his newspaper had been closed down that morning over an article about corruption. We observe the usual taboos, but rarely in one room have I encountered such a range of opinion – some work for the official state media, some for the various opposition papers – and such a working atmosphere of respect for others to voice their views. Two of my trainees from Darfur have served a year in prison.

Next to our building, the towering offices that were used by a petroleum company stand empty; it looks like the premises will be vacant for some while. The South has shut down its oil production rather than pay the fees demanded for exporting oil through Port Sudan, thus losing, apart from aid, its only source of revenue. The agreement to build a new port on the Kenyan coast through which the South will export its oil has been signed. With the loss of all that oil revenue – it was oil that funded the boom years of Khartoum – the economic crisis is going to hit hard soon.

Winter, with its deliciously cool nights and breeze-filled days, has just come to an end. But there is no spring; there's just a shift like a change of gear in a car and, with occasional relief, the long hot summer sets in. I savour the indolence I feel myself; at times there is a kind of lingering pleasure to it. At other times it is mere exhaustion.

I've already started sorting out my belongings for packing; *The White Nile*, *Imperial Vanities* and *A History of Modern Sudan* lie scattered around on the floor. There's not a lot to ship, and after a few goodbyes – and those moments of reflection in an empty flat with the bags packed by the door – I should be done. My garden beckons, with the buds unfolding of the magnolia on the lawn, and the heady scent of lilac, and the fragile blossoms of a suburban spring.

I walk out into the street, into the intense mid-day light. Below my flat, the Southern women who squatted in the empty site with their kids and sold the *araquay* that they buried in the ground have been evicted, the roof of their makeshift home demolished to guarantee a permanent departure – not so much a matter of ethnicity as the need not to upset the neighbours too much when running a shebeen.

On the pavement the men are gathered, dipping together into the dishes of *assida* with its sauce, garrulous around the woman who serves. The neem trees, in a parody of spring, shower dried leaves on to the men sitting in their shade as winter ends, and there is almost the melancholy that autumn brings.

The pizza delivery boys are washing their scooters as the Ethiopians wander back from their church in twos and threes, the women's heads covered in white muslin. The displaced from Darfur are selling phone cards and cigarettes from a chair in the street or waiting for a car to wash near the chemist's advertising Fair and Lovely. The men from Kordofan work the petrol pumps. The lads from the Gezira man the grocer shops. All over the capital there are scenes like this – the buzz of greetings, gently mocking laughter, the hands dipping into the dish together in a communal meal, the delight in living balanced with a life-time of resignation.

It'll be different when I'm home – now there's a word! – in the streets of suburbia, silent apart from the birdsong and those brief conversations with the neighbours over the hedge. The wheelie bins are emptied on alternate Fridays.

Already, even before I have left, I am beginning to feel nostalgic (I have read that the word is rooted in the Greek for returning home) not for Ireland, but for the Sudanese.

ACKNOWLEDGEMENTS

This book began as an exhibition of black and white photographs with texts, *Days by the Nile*, at the British Council Syria. I would like to thank the former director Peter Clark for encouraging me through this exhibition.

I would like to thank Mohammed Mahmoud, a native of Kassala, for his comments when I was writing the chapter 'Beneath the Holy Mountains'.

I am particularly indebted to Marie Hanson at Garnet Publishing for her sensitive editing and patience. I would also like to thank Megan Sheer for her imaginative design of photographs and text.

It was the warm hospitality of the Sudanese that made my travels so rewarding. My thanks to those I met on the road, and to those who invited me for tea under the neem trees. They were generous companions.

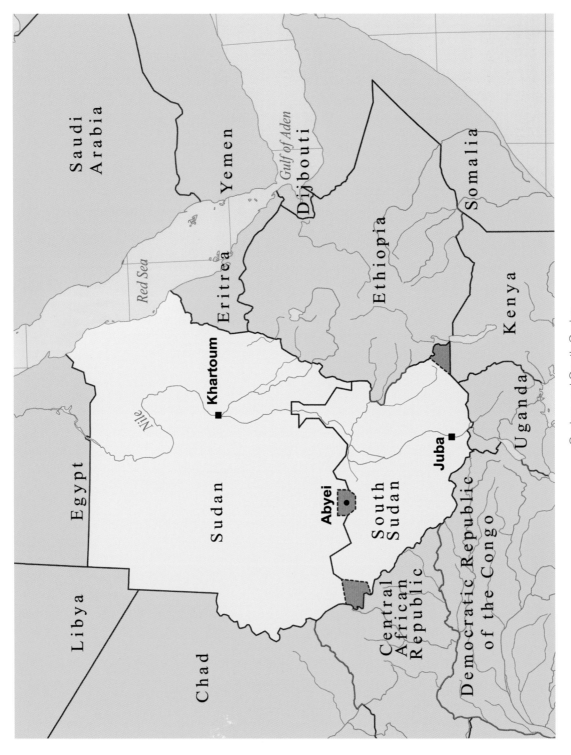

Sudan and South Sudan

GLOSSARY

abeed: slaves

Adarawb: nickname for a Beja tribesman

amjad: small minibus functioning as a taxi

angarib: traditional low wooden bed

araquay: traditional alcoholic spirit made from dates

arraqi: light, white informal robe worn by men

assida: staple food with the consistency of thick porridge

awlad al-baher: the people of the river

bamber: traditional low stool

baraka: blessing; the spiritual power believed to reside in holy places or persons

dhikar: Sufi ceremony of remembering God

dom: palm-like tree with a hard fruit

al-fatiha: opening verses of the Quran

finjan: small cup with no handle, for coffee

fuul: brown fava beans

haboub: dust storm

hajj: pilgrimage to Mecca

halal: lawful or permitted in Islamic law

haram: forbidden in Islamic law

imma: turban

inshallah: God willing

jabina: small metal pot for coffee

jallabi: 'Arab' trader in the South

jalous: mixture of dung and straw used for making walls

jebbel: mountain

jelabiyah: loose white robe worn by men

jenoubi: a Southerner

jinn: spirits believed by Muslims to have free will and to influence humanity

khawaja: 'white' foreigner

kuffar: 'unbelievers'

laconda: downmarket hotel

marissah: local beer

mulid: festival celebrating the Prophet's birthday

rickshaw: motorised rickshaw

rokuba: straw shelter

rutaana: indigenous, unwritten language

shamasha: street children; young delinquents

sharia: Islamic law

shebab: youths; the lads

sheesha: pipe for smoking, the smoke being cooled through water

sirwal: loose white trousers, often worn as an undergarment

suq: market place

tambour: traditional stringed instrument

tariqah: Sufi brotherhood

tobe: woman's robe

tukkul: thatched hut

wadi: valley that floods seasonally

zeer: clay pot for cooling water

INDEX